Advanced Sheet Metal Fabrication

Timothy Remus

Published by:
Wolfgang Publications Inc.
217 Second Street North
Stillwater, MN 55082
www.wolfpub.com

First published in 2003 by Wolfgang Publications Inc.,
217 Second Street North, Stillwater MN 55082

ISBN number: 1-929133-12-X

Printed and bound in the China

Advanced Sheet Metal Fabrication

Introduction

There's been a renaissance. A re-birth of interest in the art of metal shaping. Twenty years ago there were only a handful of men and women with the skill to make a fender or a complete motorcycle gas tank. Not very many people knew how and not very many were trying to learn. Metal shaping was seen as a black art, something that some people, old-world types especially, simply "knew" how to do.

The situation today couldn't be more different. Not only are people eager to learn, they have a variety of tools to do so. Classes are offered by Ron Covell, Fay Butler and Ron Fournier to mention only three, that range from beginning to advanced metal working. Videos, often from the same craftsmen, cover every metal working topic imaginable. The thirst for knowledge is intense and shows no sign of letting up.

And it's that thirst for knowledge that best describes the reason we assembled this new book. Our other fabrication book, *Sheet Metal Fabrication*, could be called Sheet Metal Work 101. Though some of the sequences in that book used power tools, the emphasis is on hand work and the basics of metal shaping.

Because that book was well received we now bring you *Advanced Sheet Metal Fabrication*. No longer a "101" or introductory book, *Advanced*

Sheet Metal Fabrication brings you projects that are, well, more advanced. Instead of a single shape made from one piece of aluminum or steel, this book involves the fabrication of fenders and gas tanks made up of multiple panels, each of which must be shaped before being welded to the others to create a whole.

Another important part of fabricating more complex shapes is the use of a buck. The Craig Naff and Rob Roehl projects included here include the fabrication of multi-piece projects – built with the aid of a elaborate buck.

Think of this new book as a documentary, documenting six projects from the paper drawing to the metal finishing. All performed by craftsmen with over a century of collective experience. What you have in your hands is another tool. The rest is up to you.

The story was told to me years ago that when they made plans to renovate the Statue of Liberty they needed seven sheet metal craftsmen with the skills to recreate many of the Lady's exterior panels. Skilled workers were so few and far between in this country that four of the seven had to come from Europe. I'd like to think that if that same project were undertaken today, all seven could be easily found in the US of A. Now there's something we can all be proud of.

Acknowledgements

When it comes to my "thank yous" I'd like to start with the six primary metal workers seen in the book, listed here in no particular order:

Craig Naff
Rob Roehl
Ron Covell
Fay Butler
Mike Pavletic
Bob Munroe

Each allowed me (or my photographer) into their shop, slowed down or stopped the process as necessary for the camera, and were generally as accommodating as possible.

Though he's not seen here it seems appropriate to thank the man who first showed me the incredible things that could be done with a plate of sheet steel in the right hands. It was Steve Davis who kindled my appreciation for this art form, an appreciation and sense of wonder that remain to this day.

There are some of the other usual suspects to thank as well. This list includes Arlen Ness for making the rocket bike project available and Jonathan Gold for taking the photos. Also Donnie Smith, for his help in making the gas tank sequence possible.

Neal Letouneau doesn't quite have his new hammer finished yet, but that doesn't mean he didn't help with the book. (Maybe for book three?) And then there's Bill Hacker at Yoder and James Hervatin at Precision Metal Fab & Machine.

Thanks for the cover design goes to Mikey Urseth. For doing the layout and massaging all those hundreds of pictures I tip my hat to Jacki Mitchell.

I have to close by thanking Mary Lanz, my lovely and talented wife. I promise to give up working nights and weekends - at least until the start of the next book project.

In This Issue

The Air Planishing Hammer Handbook is part of an emerging line of books and tools developed and brought to market by Fay Butler.

The professor of power hammers, Fay Butler divides his time between fabrication, in-house seminars, and consulting/teaching for a variety of American companies. Most of his in-shop seminars are done for only three students. This time, however, he's done a detailed seminar for thousands of students, all the men and women who read this book.

Thanks to Ron Covell, hundreds of (mostly) men are off on new careers as metal fabricators with a whole new set of personal tools. Thanks also to Ron, this book contains a detailed sequence on shaping by hand and with the English wheel.

In This Issue

An experienced body man, Mike Pavletic (below) got tired of working "for the man," fifteen years ago and moved to a small shop at home. Between then and now, Mike erected a new shop building and made the transition from high-end body work to metal shaping. It's a metal shaping project, the repair of an old AlfaRomeo body, that he's chosen to share with the rest of us.

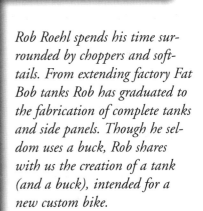

Bob Munroe is an unsung hero from the world of custom motorcycles. Working with hand tools and a wheel, Bob shapes for the world's best known motorcycle customizer, Arlen Ness. Bob is responsible for nearly thirty years worth of incredible sheet metal, and the short sequence about Arlen's latest turbine-powered motorcycle.
J. Gold

Rob Roehl spends his time surrounded by choppers and softtails. From extending factory Fat Bob tanks Rob has graduated to the fabrication of complete tanks and side panels. Though he seldom uses a buck, Rob shares with us the creation of a tank (and a buck), intended for a new custom bike.

Left, Craig Naff's work while in the Boyd Coddington shop really "put him on the map." Which is not to say he's been idle since moving home to his own shop in Virginia. Though there's often a Ferrari in the shop for panel replacement, most of Craig's work is street rod and restoration work. And it's a restoration project, the creation of a new fender, that Craig shares with us for this book.

Chapter One

Hammer History

From Plowshares (and Swords) to Body Panels

Power hammers are such an essential part of metal forming and of this book that it seemed only logical to spend a little time talking about how they originated and where the modern craftsman might find a power hammer to buy, or at least parts for some of the old standards.

AN ABBREVIATED HISTORY OF POWER HAMMERS

The two names that come up most often when people speak of serious power hammers are

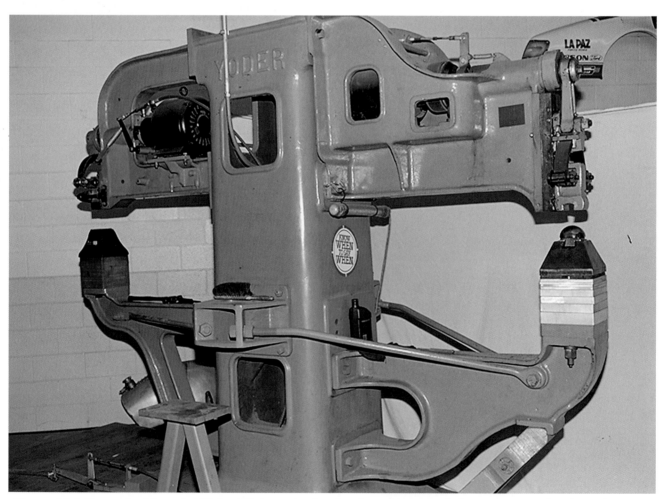

The real McCoy, a double-ended Yoder. With two ends a hard-working metal shaper can put shrinking dies on one and stretching dies on the other, or two slightly different stretching dies on either end.

Pettingell and Yoder, which is not to say that either one of these machines was the first or the most successful power hammer on the market.

The first power hammers were used for forming and forging, seldom for what we call shaping. As early as the sixteenth century (and probably earlier) mechanized hammers were used for drawing out shapes in iron. The earliest hammers were simple "helve" designs, really nothing more than a hammer head on the end of a lever. The arm was raised and then released by a simple mechanical linkage. As the mechanical revolution progressed, more efficient crank-operated, vertically oriented hammers came to market. By applying the power and speed of a power hammer to a set of closed dies, forgings could be manufactured on an economical basis.

Power hammers tend to be made from huge, heavy cast parts. Without all that mass, there's no way the structure can withstand the incessant pounding and inherent vibrations. Early advancements in power hammers involved not just speed or size, but a means of isolating the hammer and drive mechanism from the vibrations. Atmospheric and pneumatic hammers

Part of the Yoder's beauty is the ease with which the length of the stroke can be adjusted.

attempted to isolate the structure from the blows of the ram by attaching the ram to a piston contained in a cylinder. The simplest atmospheric hammer lifted the ram and piston, which created a vacuum under the piston. When the ram was released or tripped, the vacuum added force to the descending piston and ram, which was no longer connected directly to the structure of the machine.

Die support mechanism on a Yoder bears a remarkable resemblance to the assembly first patented by Mr. Shaw in 1866. The spring and strapping arrangement helps to isolate the frame from bad vibes and allows for a dead blow.

9

How to Build a "Yoder"

Q & A WITH NEAL LETOURNEAU

Neal, tell us first how you decided to build a Yoder?

It's all about work, it does more work than you can do alone. More work in a shorter period of time

Why not just buy one?

They're hard to find and phenomenally expensive. Plus if I build one I can update the drive system for more efficiency and less maintenance.

Where did you start on this quest?

I called Yoder, got Bill Hacker on the phone, he told me about Clay Cook and Jim Hervatin (see Sources). Jim built his own Yoder so I called him and asked him some questions. He let me drive down and dimension his machine, he got me started. I bought the bottom tool post, connecting rod, spring mount and the clutch from Jim. Everything else I came up with on my own.

Do they still make Yoder hammers?

They've only made one hammer in the last 20 years, and that was for a Korean aircraft company. Basically, they don't make them anymore because in their eyes there's no demand. They will supply parts. In fact, they mailed me prints for the LKM 90 and LK 90, the two basic model numbers. I just scaled off those prints to get what I've got.

You made some improvements in the basic design?

I'm using a sealed roller bearing instead of ball bearing on the connecting rod so there's better support and no maintenance. And I'm going to eliminate the clutch by using a DC electric motor with a foot pedal to control the speed. The direct drive makes it simpler and there's fewer parts to wear out, less maintenance. I did buy the clutch castings from Jim, and Clay Cook can line them with a Kevlar material, instead of the old brake lining material or whatever they used originally, but I think direct drive is the way to go.

How much do you have invested in the new hammer?

To date I've spent about 2000 dollars, and I will probably have 5000 or 6000 in it when I'm done. I did call in some favors from friends for the machining but otherwise I've done it myself.

How did you make the arms and what are they made from?

The arms are made from 3/8 inch thick, cold-rolled, picked and oiled,

Jim Hervatin built this entire hammer by himself, and now sells a variety of the cast parts. To quell vibration Jim filled the center column with 3200 pounds of sand. Conventional clutches are converted to hydraulic operation.

How to Build a "Yoder"

Neal's Yoder uses arms built from 3/8 inch steel plate, all laser cut and formed in a brake. The original Yoder drawings were used, and then extended six inches.

More of Neal's Yoder-in-the-making. Cast clutch, connecting rod, lower tool support and spring are from Jim Hervatin. Rough cut shrinking dies are an extra set that Neal purchased from another metal shaper. Neal had the guides fabricated and machined based on the Yoder drawings.

mild steel. I had all the parts laser cut. All the webbing parts are 3/8 too. Basically, the parts are an H-beam. I had to "bump brake" the steel that wraps the webbing, to get it to match the radius of the center web. Eventually all those seams will be fully welded. The center column will be 24 by 24 inches, and eight feet tall, made from the same 3/8 inch material. I'm going to use a five foot base on the bottom. This one will have a little more reach, 6 inches deeper than the original, just so you can get in there with bigger pieces.

So could anybody do this?

Anybody with the ability to do the machine work and welding. You need to be patient, you can't be in a hurry. What you're trying to duplicate is a big, heavy cast piece. It's big and clunky and heavy for a reason. If you can get parts flame cut or laser cut that helps too. Part of this I figured out just by calling around. Scott Knight was very helpful, Fay was nice, Jim answered questions and then let me drive down to see his hammer. It's a matter of finding the right people.

No, it's not a power hammer. Yet, most shapers agree that when it comes to buying power tools, a Pullmax is one of the best investments you can make.

shoes or plow shares or work a set of closed dies.

"When the country made the transition from carriages to autos, they discovered a need for a more durable body," explains Fay Butler. "Amesbury, Massachusetts was the Detroit of the carriage industry at that time. The Pettingell company was located there and supplied the carriage companies with wood-working equipment." As the industry made the transition from carriages to automobiles, and from wood to steel, it was only

Crank-operated hammers added speed to the process but the constant vibrations shortened the life of the mechanical linkage. Inventors began to experiment with springs as a means of isolating the ram from the rest of the machine, but it wasn't until Thomas Shaw tried using a semi-elliptical spring and leather strapping that the modern ram support mechanism was invented. Douglas Freund in his book, *Pounding Out The Profits*, gives Shaw credit for the first-such spring mechanism and dates the original patent at February 27, 1866.

Mr. Shaw's drive mechanism did more than isolate the linkage from the hammer. The elliptical spring and leather strapping allowed the head to drop free onto the anvil, producing a powerful "dead blow."

"MODERN" POWER HAMMERS

If you look at one of those early Shaw designs, what you see is a spring and strapping system nearly identical to that used by both Pettingell and Yoder. While the Yoder seems to be the better known hammer, it was Pettingell that first made a crank-operated power hammer designed to shape sheet metal rather than horse

Though the motor is mounted up above the machine and drive to the hammer is by belt, the Pettingell is functionally very similar to the Yoder. Available in a variety of sizes, this is one of the largest hammers that Pettingell sold.

natural that Pettingell would continue to supply the evolving industry with tooling they needed for the new materials and manufacturing processes.

To quote Fay again, "The power hammer they developed evolved from the blacksmith hammer. Compared to a blacksmith hammer it had more throat and more speed. At one time they were a huge company, building power and hand rotary beading machnines, and all kinds of equipment. The Yoder design evolved from the Pettingell design. Yoder was successful at getting a lot of government contracts. Almost all the Yoders you see now are military surplus though some come from aircraft companies. Pettingell sold hammers primarily to automobile-related companies."

CURRENT POWER HAMMER OPTIONS

Bill Hacker, long-time employee of Yoder, confirms what Fay has to say about the Yoder hammers. "We must have sold at least a two thousand Yoders during the Second World War. I remember we had them lined up in the main bay being assembled and there were always 25 or 30 there at any one time. But the sales tapered off in the later 1940s and early 1950s."

"The government bought a lot of those, the rest went to companies like Boeing and Douglas and all the rest. The last one we sold was about five or six years ago, it went to a Korean aircraft company and cost $50,000, plus extra for the dies."

Current options for shapers and fabricators looking for a power hammer include used Yoders, parts for which can still be obtained from Yoder or

from Jim Hervatin in Missouri. In fact, Jim will sell you many of the rough-castings you need for the mechanical end of a Yoder. Used Pettingels are also available though there doesn't seem to be an underground of enthusiasts producing replacement parts.

A complete power hammer kit is available from Cal Davis, classes are offered as well. And as we go to press Loren Richards confirms that he is working on a power hammer that will be part of a new line of metal shaping tools. Finally, don't neglect to check out the tool offerings found on metalshapers.org

Whether you buy a real Yoder and do a lengthy restoration, or a new kit from Cal Davis, will depend on your budget for both time and money, and your mechanical aptitude. The important thing isn't which one you buy, but rather that you take the time to decide whether or not one of these labor savers is right for your shop. Called the "helper with no bad habits" a power hammer can shrink or stretch - and do it quicker than a dozen shapers working by hand.

Built by Loren Richards for Rob Roehl, this small hammer is a prototype for a new line of power tools designed to be both powerful and space efficient.

Mini Indy Roadster

Half a Half-Midget in Aluminum

In this sequence we follow along as Ron Covell creates the rear body section for a small "half-midget" car. This car is a personal project and not necessarily legal for any particular class of racing. Ron calls it a "half-midget" car because it's bigger than a legal quarter-midget car.

The material being used is aluminum, 3003, H14, .063 inch thick. As Ron explains, "It has a good balance of formability and strength. It's thick enough that you can do some filing and not hurt

Here we see the finished "half midget" car, built from scratch from 3003 aluminum. This is a good project, as each half of the rear body section is made up of three panels (plus the bottom). Fabricating the individual panels forces Ron to use a wide array of tools and techniques, not all of which are the same from one side to the other.

the strength. I've built some race car bodies with .050 but you have to be really careful if you do any filing. Some old Italian race cars were made with .040, but with a race car it's not uncommon for them to end up in the hay bales. And it's really hard to repair those bodies because the metal is so thin to begin with."

"The old Italian cars were crafted from panels that were formed by hand. And yes, they were formed in tree stumps just like we've all heard. Each craftsman would have a hollowed out tree stump and they would just wail away into those stumps until they got the rough shape on a particular panel. I got to tour some of those facilities in the mid-'60s. But that has all changed now. The exotic cars were all hand made in the 1960s, but now those cars are made from pressings or composites."

THE PATTERN

The project starts by making the buck, which is already built in this case. Typically before you can make a buck you need to know what the part is going to look like, you need a good drawing or a blue print. Ron built this buck pretty much by eye, but he might have used something like the original Kurtis blueprint which he owns (not shown).

As Ron gets down to business he runs a thin metal rod along the area of greatest curvature, explaining as he does, "You want to spread the difficulty between the two pieces instead of making one part really, really hard to make and the other one easy. What you're doing is balancing the difficulty of shaping each piece against the difficulty of welding all those pieces together. For example, a VW body could be made up of a thousand small pieces, each piece would be easy to make but the welding and distortion would be enormous. To take it to the other extreme, making the body from one piece, would be ridiculous."

Note: 1/8 inch diameter steel rod is used throughout this sequence instead of welding rod so it will show up better in the photos.

Back to the body at hand. Ron makes a mark on the buck to show where the edge of the metal pieces is going to be. Then he moves the rod to the bottom of the buck and marks that area in the same way. The buck itself is made from medium

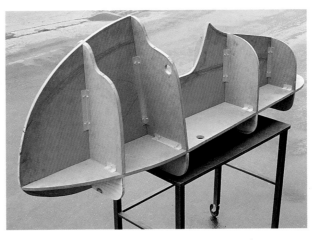

Ron already had a buck for the project, so he can start right in with the layout of the panels.

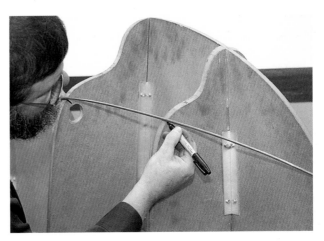

The location of the seams is marked on the buck. Ron likes to place these in the area of maximum shape.

The patterns are made from light chip board, which Ron positions over the buck.

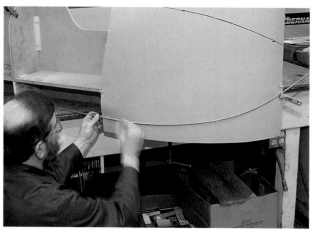

With the help of a steel rod, Ron marks the seam that will separate the side of the car from the bottom.

Much of the cutting is done with a Beverly shear.

With the chip board pinned to the buck, Ron cuts along the marked seams.

The initial shaping is done by hand on the bench...

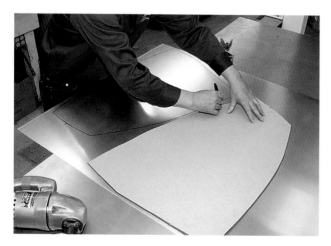

Then the outline is transferred to a piece of .063 inch aluminum.

...followed by the first of many test fits.

density fiberboard, a material Ron is quick to recommend. "The MDF has a number of advantages over other similar materials. Plywood has rough edges where it's been cut, there may be voids in the material and the density is not uniform. The MDF is uniform and you don't get splinters and it doesn't kill the edge on your cutting tools like particle board does. I hold the paper on the buck with big push-pins, with MDF the pins can be pushed into the buck, instead of being driven in with a hammer. Most commonly I use 1/2 inch, sometimes if you're going to do hammering on it I might go to 3/4 inch fiberboard."

Time now to cut out the pattern, Ron holds the pattern paper onto the form and cuts it a bit oversize. Next he transfers marks on the buck to the pattern paper. This pattern paper is chip board. Then he traces out the curves on the chip board, for both the top and the bottom. Ron doesn't cut right on the line, "I give myself about a quarter inch extra," says Ron.

START THE METAL WORK

Ron marks out the metal using the pattern. It's worth mentioning that you might as well cut out the other side at the same time. An electric shear is used at this stage because it's a fast way to do the first cut, but for the final cut he often uses a Beverly shear or a hand shear.

"To de-burr the edge I use a flat file," says Ron. "I always pull the file toward me and that's for two reasons: First, if you push the file when you're working on sheet metal it will often chatter, but by pulling on the file it hardly ever chatters. And second, when you're pushing the file toward the metal you run the risk of jamming your hand up against the sharp edge if you slip. This way if I slip my hand is moving away from the edge, not toward it."

Next, he puts the gradual over-all shape into the part. This is done before annealing the edges. This initial shaping is done freehand, followed by a test fit. "If I over bend it I put it on the table and push down on either side, the neat thing about this is it does most of the unbending at the point of contact with the table so you have real good control."

Small adjustments to the curvature of the side panel can be made on the bench.

The panel will need more work on the top and bottom, but first Ron gets the basic shape to fit the buck.

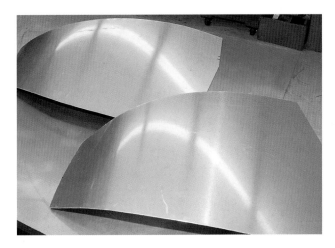

Because the panels are mirror images of each other, it's a good idea to cut and do the initial shaping to both panels before moving on.

Appealing Annealing

Step 1. Adjust the torch to a pure acetylene flame and "dirty" a three inch band along the edges of the aluminum.

Step 2. Re-adjust the torch to a standard blue flame and heat the edge just hot enough to burn off the soot.

Step 3. Repeat step two. The soot burns off at 800 degrees but aluminum metals at 1200 so you have to be careful to keep the torch moving so you don't overheat the metal.

Annealing is the process of bringing the metal back to a dead-soft condition. In the case of this aluminum sheet, it came in a half-hard condition (H14). Ron's goal is to eliminate that hardening before he starts the shaping. Sometimes annealing is used in the middle of a project to eliminate the "work hardening" that occurs as a piece is shaped and shaped and shaped. In any case, it's a useful skill to add to your bag of tricks so follow along as Ron does this demonstration.

Ron starts the process by bending the panel, explaining as he does, "I curve the parts first because the shape helps eliminate most warpage. If you anneal something that is dead flat it won't be flat when you're finished. Here we need to curl the edges, not the middle, so I'm only going to soften it along the edges."

Ron likes to elevate the part on the bench, simply so he doesn't get the acetylene soot on the table and eliminates the clean up afterwards. Ron puts a layer of soot along a three inch wide band with a pure acetylene flame. The only purpose of the black layer of soot is to act as a temperature indicator. Once he has the piece sufficiently "dirty" Ron adjusts the flame on the torch to a standard neutral flame and heats up the edge of the metal - just enough to burn off the soot. Any remaining soot dusts off fairly easily. Then Ron quenches the piece.

"I quench the pieces when I'm done," says Ron. "This is a non-heat-treatable alloy, so the quenching won't change the properties of the material, but with some alloys you might have to be more careful, they may become brittle."

Now Ron starts to curl the edges down with the shrinker. A process that goes faster and easier than it would have otherwise - if Ron hadn't taken the time to anneal the edge. And that's what it's all about.

"I put the initial shape into the parts first because the shape helps eliminate most warpage that might occur later when the part is annealed. Here we need to curl the edges, not the middle, so I only soften it along the edges."

Ron puts a layer of soot along the edge as described in the side-bar, then adjusts the torch to a more typical blue-white flame and burns off the soot before quenching the piece in water.

Now we need to curl the edges down and the first step in that process is to shrink the edge. The small shrinker shown here is available from Covell and you can interchange the jaws to make it a stretcher as well. The goal is to curve the edges over to match the shape of the buck. "I shrink the edge before I do anything else. What you see is a faceted series of angles on the piece we're shrinking. Once we have the edge positioned where we want it, then we will shape the metal farther in. This is the more efficient way to do it I think."

Ron shrinks across both long edges with the small shrinker. Note how the piece has picked up shape overall from the edge shrinking. Ron flattens it a bit on the table. There's a linkage between the front-to-back shape and the top-to-bottom shape. "So I decreased the curve front to back which increases the curvature top to bottom."

Ron explains that the effects of the shrinking stretch (no pun intended) well beyond the one-inch reach of the jaws. "I've only used one tool and we've created a dramatic amount of shape much deeper than the one inch that the jaws of the tool reach. You don't need tons of tools to create a lot of shape. While we're certainly not done, that one tool has gotten us a long long way toward the final shape." Note the photos and how the effect of the shrinker reaches as far as three inches in from the edge.

The next step is to check the shape on the buck, "I'm looking at how close the part matches the stations on the buck," says Ron. "We are within about a quarter inch at this point. It has a kind of faceted effect, flat at the edge and then a high crown area. The goal will be to make it a more gradual curve." Note the before picture of the curve at the edge of the metal.

After annealing the two side panels Ron starts shrinking along both edges.

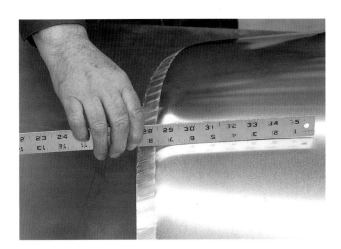

The effect of the shrinking goes well past the actual reach of the jaws and adds crown to the whole piece.

Before doing a test fit Ron shrinks along the very back edge as well.

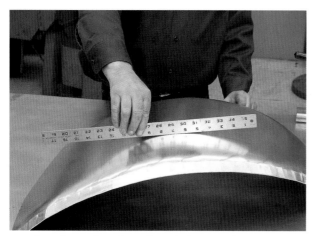

By shrinking the edges the whole piece has arched up.

Though the edges need a little work, the test fit shows the piece to be quite close.

Here Ron opens up the piece. Though by reducing the crown end-to-end, Ron has actually increased the amount of crown top-to-bottom...

This contour tool can be used to check or document any shape, or to do before-and-after checking of a small area.

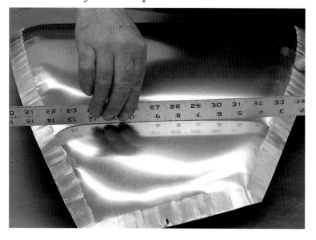

...as is seen here with the ruler.

To create a more rounded edge to the panel, Ron works the area over a dolly mounted in the vise.

To create a more gradual curve Ron starts working the edge of the panel with a slap hammer and a dolly, an old hand dolly welded to a post and mounted in the vise. "I like the slap hammer," explains Ron, "because it covers more area than a regular hammer." It takes time to work along the edges but eventually Ron creates a nice smooth radius all along the edge of the panel.

Once the panel is a fairly good fit on the buck, it's time to punch small holes along the edges. The holes allow Ron to attach the panel to the buck with his heavy duty push-pins. There's still a bit of fine adjusting to do with the slap hammer, working right against the buck. At this point both side panels are shaped and mounted on the buck, with an area of overlap at the back that still needs to be trimmed.

"Now I will establish a centerline for the trimming," explains Ron. This is actually a two-step process. Tape is used first to establish the center line of the outside panel. Then after trimming that panel and re-attaching it to the buck, Ron carefully scribes a line where the "outside" panel meets the inside. Finally the inside panel is removed and carefully trimmed with shears. Once both panels are butted together on the buck it's time to start the tack welding process.

Welding

For welding aluminum like this Ron likes to use 1/16 inch, #1100 rod. The TIG welder is set as follows: alternating current, high frequency control on continuous, medium heat range, flowing 18 CFH of argon. The tungsten used here is a 2% thoriated tungsten 3/32 inch in diameter. According to Ron, "the books say you should use pure tungsten. But for aluminum sheet metal the 2% holds a sharp tip better and having a sharp tip allows you to focus the weld into a small area which gives you better control." Ron works the seam as he welds, to ensure the two panels stay parallel and in alignment, and that the seam stays close to the buck.

The Dirty Finger Technique

It's time now to make another pattern using what Ron calls the dirty finger technique. "First I tape butcher paper onto the buck with three pieces

Though the effect is somewhat subtle, the contour gauge shows us how Ron has softened the crown at the edge of the panel.

Now the two rear panels can be attached to the buck with pins and tape.

Scribing a cut line where the two panels meet is done by first marking the center line on the outside panel with tape.

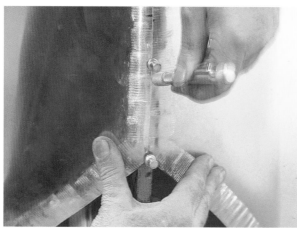

Then the outside panel is removed, trimmed and placed on the buck. Now a line can be scribed on the inside panel where the two will butt.

Ron does a little fine adjusting of the bottom edge prior to forming a paper pattern.

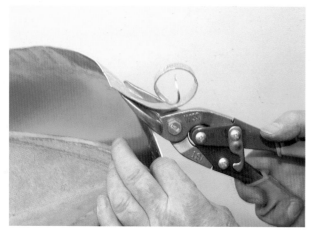

For accurate trimming it's hard to beat good aircraft shears in the hands of a patient craftsman.

The pattern is marked using Ron's famous "dirty finger technique." Fabricators with clean hands need not apply.

With a TIG welder you can get a decent tack weld while the panels are on the buck, with gas it's hard to get any kind of weld because of the wood behind the metal.

After making the paper pattern Ron folds it in half, adjusts the actual outline just slightly and then transfers the outline to the aluminum.

of tape, then I rub my dirty finger along the edge and it leaves a mark that's easy to see."

"I like to fold the pattern in half to judge its symmetry, in this case it's off about 1/2 inch. I will split the difference. That is, I find the line that is half way between the two edges and cut there. Next I draw a centerline on a piece of aluminum and then use the adjusted pattern for both halves."

Now Ron marks the aluminum, trims it first with the electric shear and then does the final trim with the hand-operated Beverly shear. The first step is to create the rough shape, then anneal it as was done before.

Once again, the shrinker is a key part of the shaping process. As Ron explains, "the shrinking is causing the piece to pick up some crown, people don't realize how far in-board the material is shaped even though the shrinker has only a one-inch throat." After the edges are passed through the shrinker it's time for a test fit and then some further adjusting with the hammer and fixed dolly. After another test fit Ron moves to a different dolly with a softer crown, "because I don't want a real sharp curve on the edge of the metal."

Another test fit shows that we need a little more angle all along the edge which is done with the first dolly and the slap hammer. Now it's rocking on the buck and the point is too far off the buck. "The area where it's hitting the buck is in the center," explains Ron, "so I need to re-contour the metal so it fits the buck better. And by shrinking on either edge close to the point it will draw the point down."

The piece needs a little further shaping at the edges, as shown in the photos. Ron spends time working the edges of both the center piece and the two side panels. Then it's time to start scribing lines. The two pieces are taped together and a putty knife is used to keep the bottom under the other pieces. "We are scribing with the bottom panel under the others," says Ron. "You could do it either way but the idea is to keep the seam in the middle of the curve." Ron spaces the tack welds evenly about 3/4 of an inch apart.

After tack welding all along one side Ron switches and starts the same process on the other

In this case the final cutting is done with the Beverly shears instead of the hand shears. The size of the aluminum panel is slightly larger than the paper pattern.

As before, the initial shape is put in the panel without any fancy tools.

The shape put into the piece in the preceding step helps prevent warpage during this annealing operation.

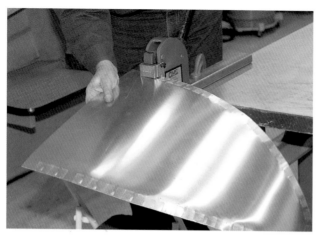

Once the edges are dead-soft, Ron can start shrinking along the perimeter of the bottom panel. Getting enough crown required two sessions on the shrinker.

The first test fit shows that with only a minimal amount of work the bottom panel is very close to final form.

Nearly any shrinker leaves a shelf or angle at the edge of the area that was in the jaws. Ron minimizes the edge with the slapper and post-dolly.

side. Because this buck is tapered towards the rear there is no danger that we won't be able to pull the rear section off after it's tacked together.

Tack welding involves a certain amount of tapping and adjusting, for times when one piece slides under the other, or doesn't quite fit. Ron explains that, "The goal for this part of the project is alignment: to make sure the two pieces are flush and to even out the surface. There are places where I drove the metal down to close the gap, but now that they are welded I need to raise those sections by going over the seams with the hammer and dolly."

Fabrication involves a certain amount of planning. Like a good pool player a fabricator needs to take each shot with an eye toward the next and the next. As Ron explains the strategy, "Before I did anything, I thought about which piece to make first and last. I made the bottom at this stage so I can reach all the seams from the inside."

When the bottom is tack welded all the way around, Ron can go ahead and finish-weld the seam. For this welding Ron uses the same settings as those noted before. "I do it all at once, continuous. If it's two pieces of mild steel with a mild crown I might move around to minimize warpage, but with aluminum and a piece with this much shape, I don't see a problem."

"Sometimes with a piece like this I fusion weld the inside of the seam as well. It looks better and it adds to the strength if there are any places that don't have full penetration. I just go in afterwards and do it with heat, I don't add any filler, I just flow together the metal that's there."

THE THREE PANELS

The three panels are now joined. For sanding the seams Ron uses soap as a lubricant, any bar soap will work. The disc is 50 grit on a standard seven inch grinder. "I have better control with the seven inch," explains Ron. "The goal at this point is to grind off any of the bead that stands up proud above the surface. You of course don't want to get carried away and grind on the metal to the point where you thin the surface."

"If you keep the sanding discs sharp you have pinpoint control as to where it's cutting. Once they get dull you loose that control. People often use the sanding discs longer than they should. "

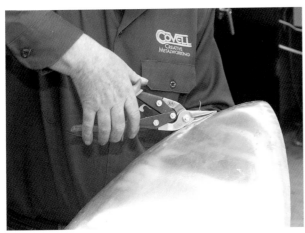

After a little more shrinking and a test fit, Ron can scribe a line where the panels overlap and trim the bottom pan to butt against the two side panels.

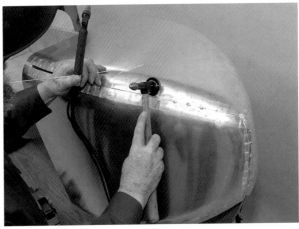

After each tack Ron does a little hammer and dolly work, to minimize the gap and keep the two edges even.

After trimming the piece is a near perfect fit. Visible gaps can be adjusted slightly as Ron does the tack welding.

Here you can see how Ron holds the bottom panel up tight against the side as he does a tack weld.

Tack welding starts at the point and moves down either side.

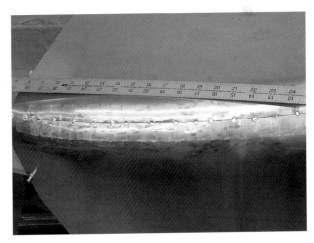

The tack welds are spaced evenly, less than an inch apart. Note the tight gap and the nice way the two edges meet.

Before starting on the final welding Ron works the hammer and dolly along the entire seam.

...so Ron can come back and do the final welding in one continuous pass.

Low spots need to be raised with a small hammer working from inside, checking the progress after each hammer blow.

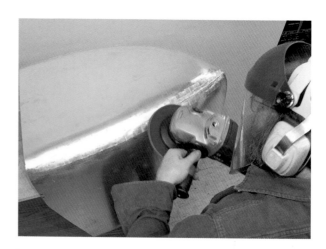

Prior to more hand work, Ron runs a grinder over the seam to eliminate most of the additional weld material.

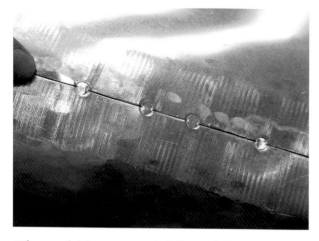

The careful hammer and dolly work leaves the seam in near-perfect alignment...

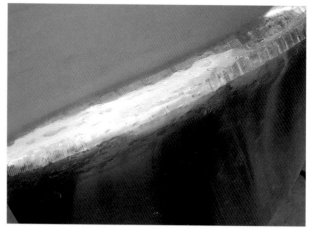

The seven inch grinder and 50 grit disc leave the seam in nice condition, requiring only a bit of finish work to be done later.

Now Ron cuts the weld at the rear of the body so he can pull the two panels together slightly and close up the gap. Ron adjusts the top edge a little so it pulls in tighter against the buck.

PLANNING AND FABRICATION FOR THE UPPER BODY PANELS.

Ron starts planning this section by deciding to make the upper body from four separate pieces of aluminum. "I hold the paper up where it seems to want to lie," says Ron. "That way the paper, and ultimately the metal, won't have to move so very far. Then I lock it in place with the push pins. Once it's positioned the trick is to push the top down until it meets the center station of the buck. Then I mark it on the far side of the center station (the one running front to rear). That station material is 1/2 inch thick so my line will be 1/4 inch over the front-to-rear center line, making it a little oversize."

Now Ron runs the rod along through the middle (or bottom) of the concave section, the area of maximum shape. He marks that and cuts it out, then cuts out a mirror image for the other side.

Time now to cut out the parts from more of our .063 inch aluminum. After cutting the rough shape Ron trims the parts on the Beverly shear and de-burrs the edge. Both panels are annealed completely, not just at the edges.

The process used to shape these upper panels is much different that that used for the bigger side panels. As Ron explains,"These panels have a lot of shape over every square inch, so I rough shape them with a mallet and sandbag. The first hits are in a line, this is where the metal needs to stretch the most."

Note the change in side to side curvature after the piece is straightened out. Now Ron tries it on the car, it's not a bad fit but we need more of the same. After the second round of mallet and bag work Ron straightens it again and again we get a huge jump in the amount of side to side curvature. Eventually Ron gets it to the point where it has enough overall shape though the surface looks like a series of walnuts. Ron switches from a sand bag to a wood block and then to the post dolly and a slap hammer.

Before starting on the upper panels Ron cuts the rear seam at the top and pulls the two panels tighter together.

The edge of the two side panels must also be adjusted to better meet the new upper panels.

Now it's time to create paper patterns for the upper panels.

After studying the project Ron decides to make the upper panels from two pieces (per side) with a seam along the concave area.

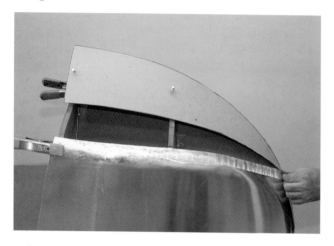

After cutting along the seam Ron has a template of the unshaped upper panel...

...and can go ahead and cut another piece of aluminum.

For the lower part of the panel Ron uses a hammer and a dolly that is much less crowned than the other dolly on the post. Another test fit shows that the panel follows the shape of the buck very well, though we haven't yet started to roll the lower edge. To create the lower roll Ron brings out his secret tool. The edge rolls quite easily against the tube and after only one series of hits the test fit looks pretty good.

Ron does a little more work with the slap hammer against the tube. "The trick," explains Ron, "is to use a found item that has exactly the right radius. You just hit the metal until it bottoms out against the tube, and then it takes on the shape of the tube."

The same shaping procedure is used for the mirror-image panel, though Ron uses the bench-top English wheel to smooth out the surface. Ron uses very little pressure on the wheels, and just moves across the piece the way you would mow a lawn, with very little overlap between one pass and the one next to it. Working with the wheel is fast and the results are smoother than what you get with a hammer and dolly.

Ron does one more series of passes through the wheel, working at a 30 or 40 degree angle to the first. "This is like block sanding," explains Ron. "You change the angle so you make the panel smooth without leaving a pattern." Again, the lower edge is formed against the pipe.

With the two halves of the headrest formed (welding will happen later) Ron cuts another piece of chip board for the middle panel and transfers the measurements to the aluminum. "If you work only with the wheel you might not need to anneal the metal," explains Ron. "The wheel has enough power to move the metal without annealing, but if you work with hand tools then the annealing really helps."

After the center piece is partly formed on the wheel Ron decides to scribe and trim it, and weld it to the top piece. Then finish the forming after it is welded to the left half of the headrest. "There is no point in shaping metal that you are eventually going to trim off," explains Ron.

The initial shaping of the upper piece is done with nothing fancier than a plastic mallet...

To achieve more crown Ron goes back to the mallet and sand bag.

...which causes the panel to curl more than Ron would like.

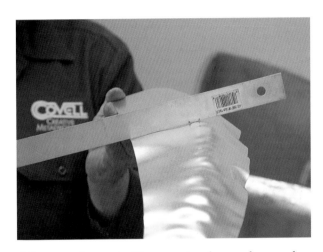

The second round of hammering leaves the panel with a sharp V shape.

After Ron eliminates the curl he's left with the beginnings of a crowned panel.

A test fit shows Ron how far he's come - and how far he still has to go.

At this point the piece has enough shape but needs smoothing, which is done by working against a piece of wood instead of the bag.

Ron does a test fit prior to more finishing work...

...done with a slap hammer and the post dolly.

MORE WELDING

The welding is done off the buck. Ron has witness marks where the two panels line up and will start welding there. It would seem difficult to weld the two panels off the buck and have them fit correctly. But Ron explains that, "They only fit together one way, if you have them the wrong way there's a gap. So it's easy to get them aligned correctly for welding."

The two pieces are joined by tack welds, Ron carefully hammers each one, explaining, "the first thing I'm after as I go through this process is the alignment of the two pieces of metal and the second thing is the contour."

With the two pieces aligned and exhibiting a nice contour Ron goes ahead with the final welding. "I'm trying something new. Instead of welding from the outside of the skin and then fusion welding the inside, I'm going to weld on the inside of the two panels and then fusion weld the outside. It should give us a smaller bead on the outside to clean up."

Ron flattens the bead with the planishing hammer "for speed" and then finishes the hard-to-reach areas with a hammer working over the piece of tubing, explaining, "I could have done the whole thing by hand but it would have taken a lot longer." The seam is flat and now Ron goes on to the other side.

The only real difference in the creation of the middle panel for the right side is the fact that Ron decided to anneal it prior to shaping, "because the other one was too much of a battle."

Once Ron has the two panels joined to make a complete right side upper section, it's time to weld the two upper body halves together. This nearly-final step in the process starts as Ron attaches the left side upper panels to the buck with stick pins and then runs a centerline with a piece of masking tape. The left side panel is trimmed along the centerline and set back on the buck. Next the right side is set on the buck, with the edge set underneath the left side panel. Now a line is scribed in the right side panel, the panel is removed and trimmed, and the two pieces are tack welded off the buck. Ron does it this way, "so I can get that top seam into the planishing hammer and save

It's a slow process but each test fits shows further progress.

...which is shaped by rolling the aluminum against a homemade fixture with the correct radius.

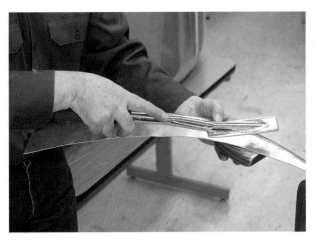

The last of the "walnuts" are eliminated with the slap hammer and dolly.

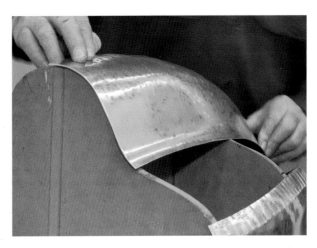

The final check shows a very nice panel - formed completely with hand tools.

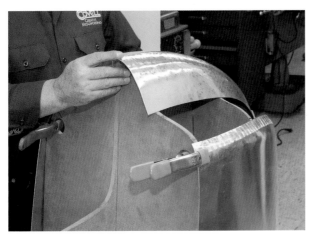

The piece is looking pretty nice, though Ron still needs to begin forming the concave section...

Which means it's time now to start on the upper panel for the right side.

After achieving enough shape by working with mallet and sand bag, Ron decides to smooth the surface with the wheel. "You control how much you raise the metal by adjusting the pressure on the wheels. Here we keep the pressure low."

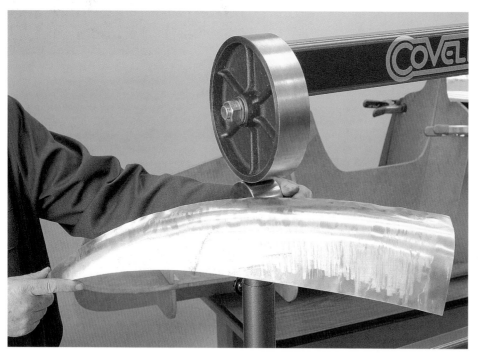

"I'm using an 8-1/2 inch radius lower wheel, a radius that matches the shape of the part. By rolling the short way I'm able to use a low-crown wheel."

myself a bunch of time." By tack welding off the buck Ron is able to move the two pieces around to keep the joint nice and tight at the point of each tack weld. Once the seam is tack welded and massaged over a dolly the final welding can begin. This is done conventionally with the bead on the outside and a fusion weld along the inside.

The top section is now welded into one unit. Ron finished the top seam in two ways. Closer to the front he used the English wheel which did a great job of flattening the seam. "I did this without grinding the bead first, so that extra metal has to go someplace. In this situation it raised the top of the headrest slightly, which is OK because the fit against the buck was a little tight to begin with. Normally I would probably grind the bead first, then run it through the wheel."

For the tail-end of the body section Ron knocked the bead down with a sander in a more conventional fashion, followed with a few passes through the planishing hammer.

Ron attaches the new top section to the buck with two dry-wall screws. Once attached to the buck he scribes a line, pulls the section off the buck and trims the lower section using hand shears. After trimming Ron screws the top section back onto the buck then does a little final adjusting of the metal

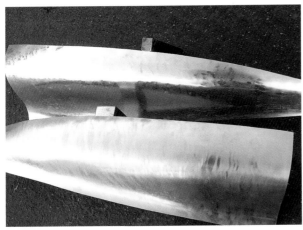

The two finished panels. Note the difference in finish between the piece that was wheeled (lower) and the one finished with hammer and dolly.

As Ron continues to work the metal he changes the angle of attack to avoid leaving any pattern in the metal.

With the upper panel clamped in place Ron marks out a pattern for the center panel.

Ron is using a higher-crown lower wheel here that allows him to wheel along the length of the panel.

The center panel is shaped entirely on the wheel, without any annealing first.

Ron starts the tack welding at one end, and closes up the gap as he moves up the seam.

Note how the two pieces come together as Ron tack welds his way up the seam.

To minimize the size of the bead Ron welded the bead on the inside of the two panels, then "flowed" the seam on the outside.

Before doing the final welding Ron puts the piece on the buck and checks the fit...

Before finishing the seam Ron knocks down the bead, which is on the inside this time.

...then carefully hammer and dollys the entire seam.

The planishing hammer speeds up the finish work.

at the edges. Now the tack welding can commence. Ron starts at the tail end with two or three tack welds, and then starts up one side and then the other. After each tack Ron adjusts the metal at the site of the tack weld and also just "downstream," Sometimes a small cut-off putty knife is used to bring the two parts back to a butted condition when one edge slips under the other. Following the tack welding it's time to peel the part off the buck, hammer and dolly both seams and then do the finish welding.

METAL FINISHING

As Ron explains, "The traditional method is to hammer every square inch of the bead until they are perfectly smooth both inside and out. Whether or not you actually finish it to that level is up to you."

The first step is to knock down the bead with the electric sander, followed by a Vixen file and some careful hammer and dolly work all along the seam. This is a process that's easier to explain through a series of photographs, and that's what we've tried to do here, starting with the proverbial "before" picture and ending with a perfectly smooth seam.

INTERVIEW, RON COVELL

Ron, can we talk a little about bucks, the different kinds of bucks and the advantages and uses of each.

There are many types of bucks. The wire type is one of my favorites. Typically they are made from steel round rod, 1/8, 3/16 or 1/4 inch diameter. What I like is, they are fast to construct, well suited to long sweeping curves and real easy to change. With wood, if you need to shave off some material that's easy, but it's cumbersome to add material. With wire, you can cut one element loose, re-contour it and re-attach it.

The bucks that most of us are familiar with are made from MDF (medium density fiberboard). The advantage to these types of bucks is that they're relatively cheap, fast to make and you can pick up as much detail as you need. The number of stations can change per the contour. That is, you use more stations where there is more shape.

Trimming and fitting the two upper halves starts as Ron marks the centerline on the left half. The process is the same as that used for the two lower side panels.

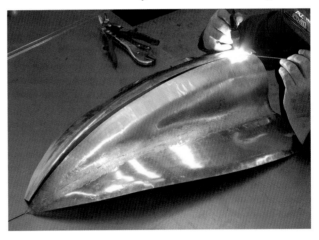

Again, tack welding starts at one end and moves along...

...with adjusting and occasional hammer and dolly work between the individual tacks.

Here you can see Ron positioning one panel so it's tight up against the other while doing another fusion weld.

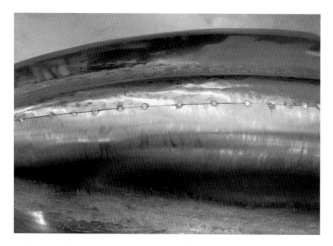

The welds are placed evenly all along the seam.

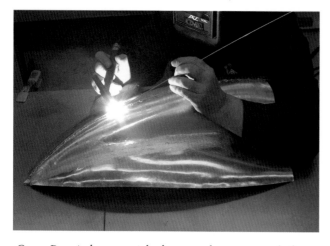

Once Ron is happy with the way the two panels fit together he can go ahead and do the finish weld in one continuous seam.

Portions of the buck can be made very rugged, so they can be hammered on.

Some people use clay, this is expensive but picks up fine detail which makes it easier to envision the overall shape. No gaps to visualize. You can read the shapes with the highest degree of accuracy.

Foam is faster, I've seen people use insulation foam from builders supply companies. That's OK but it doesn't sand or shape as easy as surfboard or urethane foams. These come in a wide range, from light to dense and can be shaped with great precision.

And there's paper mache', you can make a form quickly from chicken wire and strips of newspaper dipped in glue. You have a nice form at very low cost. A buck is generally too flimsy to hammer on. A buck is most often used as a template.

What are the skills an individual needs to develop in order to begin making more advanced shapes?

Let's just say the people with persistence pick it up. The best indicator of success is persistence, it doesn't come easy for most people. Good hand-eye coordination is paramount. In addition I would encourage them to focus on welding very early in the process. It's so essential to almost anything you do. A lot of people struggle with the welding part.

So do people need a TIG or heli-arc welder to do big sheet metal projects or is a gas outfit good enough?

Starting out with gas is what I would recommend, in time I would encourage them to get a TIG welder….. because it gives you control. Control of heat and puddle size is a real advantage. With the TIG you can make a tiny weld that's easy to finish and work, it gives you good workability of the weld area.

Advanced sheet metal means bigger more complex shapes. Can you talk about the seams? How does a person decide where to put the seams and how does he or she decide how many pieces to make an individual part out of?

Beginning metal shapers usually make things from more pieces because their skill in shaping is moderate and they would rather have the seams to deal with. As they develop more skill they often use fewer and fewer pieces. Once you have control

A small lower wheel is useful for working a tight radius. Here Ron shows how the wheel from his benchtop unit can be adapted to the full-size wheel.

The top seam too blends neatly into the panel on either side after a few passes through the wheel.

For this finishing operation Ron wants the lower wheel's radius to match that of the headrest.

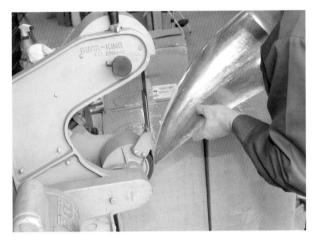

To finish the lower part of the seam Ron first grinds off the excess material...

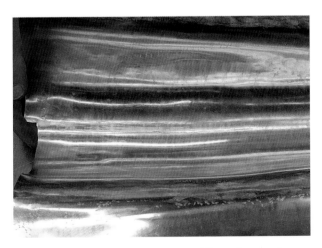

The combination of a fusion weld on the inside followed by the passes through the wheel leave the inside of the bead nearly invisible.

...and then passes the seam through the planishing hammer.

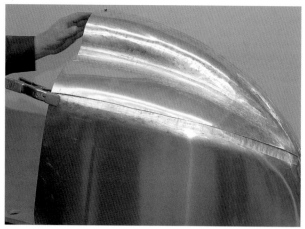

Now it's time to clamp the upper assembly to the lower.

After screwing the upper section back on the buck Ron aligns the two panels...

Then scribe a line where the two panels overlap.

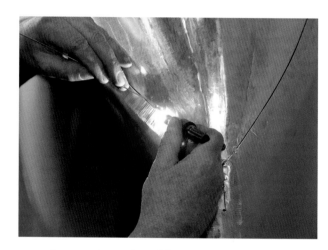

...and starts the tack welding sequence.

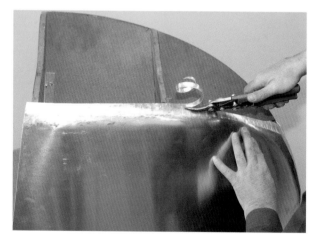

Then trimming the lower panel to create a nice butt-joint.

Occasionally Ron has to hold the putty knife in place while he does the nearby tack weld. In this careful fashion he works his way up the seam.

you can make the pieces bigger and it speeds the process. There's another benefit of fewer pieces: if you're making a '40 Ford rear fender and you make it from 6 pieces it's hard to keep the continuity of shape, or flow, after all the pieces are joined. The tools you work with make a difference too. By hand it's hard to make big pieces, but if you have a wheel or a planishing hammer then it's much easier to make larger pieces.

The overriding idea is to make the part from the smallest number of pieces that you can, consistent with your ability to shape metal. Smaller number of pieces means less warpage from welding and less weld clean up.

How should people decide where to put the seams?

You can shrink, stretch or bend a piece of metal. Every part must be made using combinations of those. Since I don't have power shrinking equipment, I can only shrink a limited amount, I can only work close to the edge. So most of the shaping I do is done by stretching. Working in that way it makes the most sense to put seams in the middle of the areas of greatest curvature.

The equipment you use has a lot to do with it. With a Pullmax that can shrink 36 inches into a panel you can do things that I simply can't, and it affects the layout of the part.

What kind of tools are needed for advanced sheet metalwork?

I would say get a TIG welder first. Next, a more sophisticated shrinking machine, to go past the limits of the one that I have, it gives you a lot more capability. Next some sophisticated way to stretch and smooth large pieces, a wheel or hammer of some kind.

What holds people back from bigger more complex projects?

People can't be afraid to make mistakes. No one's gone far in this business by doing things the same way over and over. Don't be afraid to try some new things at the risk of throwing away a few panels.

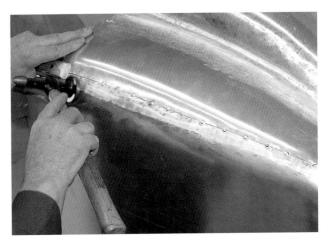

Following the tack welding Ron starts to hammer and dolly the seam.

The small grinder can be employed any where there's a blob up of metal on the inside of a tack weld, this eases the hammer and dolly work.

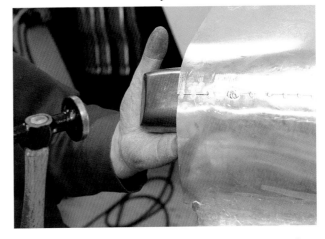

With the inside lumps out of the way it's time to finish the hammer and dolly work. Radius of dolly is close to inside radius of the seam area.

We've decided to finish the chapter with a finishing sequence. Thus the "before" picture of the seam after one pass with the electric grinder.

... which results in quite an improvement in the surface contour.

Another perspective on the before condition of this seam.

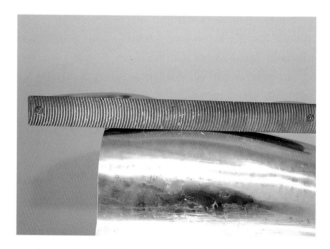

A sharp vixen file is used here for at least two reasons.

First Ron knocks down the obvious high spots and raises the low areas...

As Ron files across the same he will knock down the highs, and thereby identify the lows.

...as is shown here at this mid-point in the finishing sequence.

Note the elimination of nearly all the low spots.

Ron uses one of his own picks to raise the low areas...

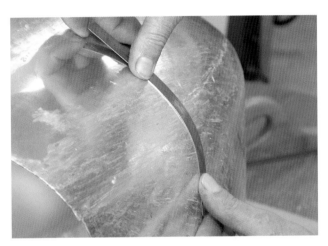

A fact that's confirmed by this side view. How far you go with the finishing, "is really up to the fabricator."

...followed by a bit more filing. Ron is careful so that the amount of material that he removes with the file is minimal.

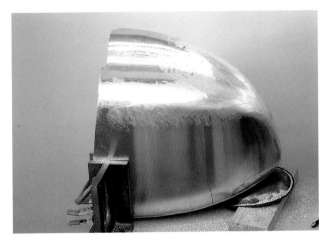

Here we have the finished body seam on a complete rear body section.

New Fairings and Old Race Cars

From the Master of Metal Shaping

Some people know in the second grade that they want to be a doctor or a firefighter. For Fay Butler there was never any choice as to his vocation. "It's all I've ever done," explains Fay. After almost 30 years of metal shaping Fay's resume includes everything from stainless steel exhaust ports for an Italian helicopter to complete car bodies, right down to the wood inner structure for the body and all of the upholstery.

Two of Fay's more recent, more typical, shaping projects are presented here: The construction of a wheel fairing assembly for a Cessna airplane and a complete front body section for a Lotus.

Fay holds the new wheel fairing half in both hands as he compares it to the original piece just behind. What made this piece hard to shape is the .050 inch 5052 H34 (half-hard) aluminum it's made from. It would have been easy if Fay could have used 1100 or 3003.

THE WHEEL FAIRING,

Seen here is the fabrication of a wheel fairing for a Cessna aircraft. This might seem a fairly easy proposition until you realize the material called for by the customer is 5052 H34 (half-hard) aluminum, a very tough and springy alloy without the soft forgiving nature of the somewhat more common 3003 aluminum. The other thing that makes this job tough is the very tight radius used on the rear corners of the housing. Fay starts the project by explaining: "The best panel is one with even tension, no material removal and true surfaces."

Fay starts with a paper pattern, held in place on the original fairing by a whole series of magnets. Wrinkles show the area where the maximum shrinking will occur. "This is made out off 5052 aluminum," explains Fay. "That's a hard material to work with, but the customer wants it that way. It has 30% more tensile strength than 3003 and it work hardens really fast."

Fay trims the paper to match the existing fairing, "I pencil the rib detail in, more as a reference than anything else," explains Fay. "Now I determine the highlight line. The highlight line defines the piece. When you shine a light on the fairing that highlight line will determine what it looks like. The highlight line is the area with the tightest radius. In this case it's a four inch radius. I make it a point to find the highlight line on almost every project. The radius gauge is a good way to determine where that highlight line is and what the radius is."

With a paper pattern in hand Fay can cut out a piece of aluminum from the sheet, then trim it to size. "I drew in the highlight line, that's where our shrinking is going to stop," says Fay. Before going any further he straightens out the edge with the planishing hammer and de-burrs the edge of the cut.

Now we set up the shrinking dies. The effect of the shrinking dies goes beyond the point where you stop, so you have to plan for that in the beginning. Fay subtracts 7/8 inch all the way 'round and creates a line. By stopping there with the die he will stop the effect of the die at the highlight line marked earlier.

Next, Fay marks the area, the corner that will get the maximum shrinkage. This is indicated by the folds on the paper pattern. Shrinking is done in the following way: one or two passes going the full depth of the line, then a few passes half and less than half way into the piece – done on either side of the first couple of deep passes.

Magnets are used (one on each side) to hold the paper in place. You could also cut small holes in the paper and tape it in place.

The areas with too much paper will also have too much metal, these are areas that will need shrinking.

"What we have is a modified box. The corners I have to tear out to make the box represent the amount of metal we have to move."

A radius gauge is used to find the area of tightest radius, which Fay marks on the paper pattern.

Fay marks the metal with both the outline and the limit of shrinking.

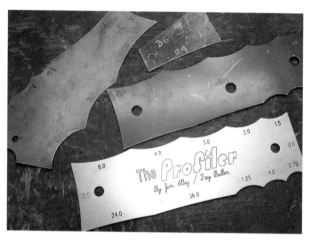

Fay's tool box contains a whole series of radius gauges, helpful in finding the highlight line or the best die to use for stretching a piece of metal.

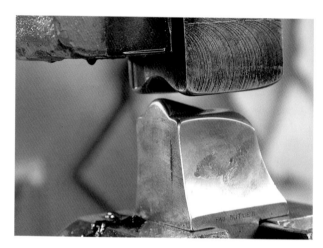

The initial shrinking is done with these thumbnail shrinking dies in the Yoder power hammer.

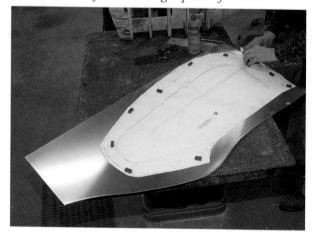

Magnets are used again to position the paper pattern on the raw 5052 aluminum sheet.

Because the effect of the shrinking die extends beyond the die itself, Fay subtracts almost an inch from the line that marks the end of shrinking.

Now Fay shrinks two areas on the top edge, each is a wedge shaped area similar to those seen on the forward corner. Following the shrinking Fay does a test fit. Followed by a little stretching in the middle of the piece with what he describes as, "a pretty flat die with a 30 or 36 inch radius." Fay starts by planishing some of the wrinkles out of the area he just ran through the shrinking dies, then does some mild stretching in the middle of the panel. Then he puts the paper back on the buck as a quick check. Fay uses the English wheel next, "I think of the wheel as a slow hammer. Here I'm using it to planish the edges slightly and to raise the metal through the center."

TEST FITTING

On this 5052 Fay recommends going slow. "You don't want to have to go back because that means extra work-hardening." And he would rather not anneal this piece as that means giving up dent resistance. Now the piece goes back on the shrinker, most of the work is done on the front corner, following the same familiar pattern: one deep draw with a series of shallower draws on either side, "when I'm shrinking I always work in a triangular pattern."

Now Fay does a little planishing on the power hammer, "I hit it pretty light, we're not doing much shaping. Actually if you hit it light, as you smooth out an uneven area you can actually shrink the metal." This material has a tremendous amount of strength; it's springy and fights back as Fay bends it into wheel-fairing form. Lots of test fits at this point. According to Fay, "when the part gets close it should only take one clamp to hold it on the wooden buck."

The corner is over-shrunk a little and needs to be stretched, and then the whole thing will fit better on the buck. The area measures four inches with the radius gauge, "but we can stretch it with a die that has a little bit bigger radius," explains Fay. Then comes a smaller shrinking die, "just to work in a smaller area," at the front of the fairing.

"You can clamp it onto the buck and then see where the tension is and figure out what to do." In this case the piece needs a little more shrinking on the top about two-thirds of the way to the back, to get the rear of the panel to pull in against the buck. "You have to be really careful that you don't create creases or sharp edges because those are stress risers and with this harder aluminum it will crack right there.

Test fittings are also thought sessions, another opportunity to figure out why the part doesn't fit the

Fay bends the sheet of aluminum into a tunnel shape as he inserts it into the Yoder, so the dies won't form a "shelf" at the end of their travel.

Fay commonly shrinks in this wedge shaped pattern, going all the way to the edge of shrinking in the center and half way or less on either side.

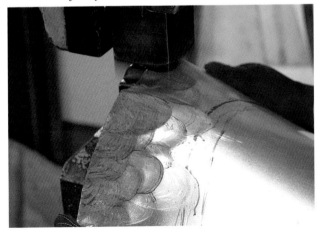

The top corner needs a lot of shrinking. Here you can see the wedge shaped pattern repeated across the wheel fairing.

The first round of shrinking leaves the wheel fairing with the beginning of the correct shape.

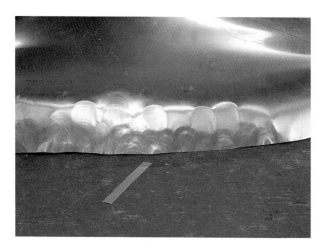

Here you see the effects of shrinking all across the top of the wheel fairing.

With stretching dies in the Yoder, Fay eliminates some of the wrinkles created by the shrinking.

buck yet, or where the piece needs to be stretched or shrunk. In this case, a little stretching at the front highlight takes tension out of the whole piece.

"I left the piece a little bigger than it needed to be," says Fay. "In case the whole thing slid too far forward. But now it's fitting pretty good and we don't need that extra material so I'm going to cut it off. It adds a lot to the effort that it takes to shape the piece." To better assess the progress Fay puts the paper pattern back on the panel, "this is just a good way to collect more information."

To illustrate just how much the shrinking has added to the aluminum's thickness, Fay works a caliper across the metal. The dial indicates an additional .005 to .009 inches of thickness all through the corner where most of the shrinking occurred. At this point the lower rear corner "isn't quite right" and is putting tension in the center of the panel. Shrinking is the answer.

We've reached the point on this project where the basic shape is determined. What comes now are hours of patient fine-tuning for all the areas that aren't quite finished. And massaging the panel to finish shaping the difficult rear corners with their tight radius.

The next "skull session" shows the rear corner to be over-shrunk, which requires a bit of stretching with a sharp die. After each stretching session Fay checks the fit and then makes notes on the outside. Different color markers are used to indicate areas that need work, in this way he is able separate new notes from old notes. At this point Fay does quite a bit of work on the upper rear corner.

Fay often uses a thin strip of light board as a "feeler gauge" to determine whether, and where, the metal is contacting the buck. When he is finally able to clamp the top of the fairing to the buck without major wrestling he pronounces that "we have a form problem, not a shape problem. If there were a shape problem I wouldn't have been able to clamp it on the buck that easily (check out Fay's interview for definitions of form and shape)."

As the piece is clamped on the buck Fay examines where it does and doesn't fit the buck and where puckers have developed. It's hard at this point to get the rear corners to come around, especially the lower rear corner.

Fay marks the highlight line at the upper rear corner, we have too much metal there and need to do a little shrinking, the shrink should never go any deeper than the highlight line. "When you pull it off the buck and change the form, to average the radiuses you analyze it again. Now you are dealing with pure shape." There is a low spot on the side, at the upper rear corner, this is another indicator that we need more shrinking along the top.

Stretch, then shrink, then clamp onto the buck and analyze again.

After the analyzing Fay installs a fairly flat stretching die and works the side along the bottom and back. This seems to take a lot of tension out of the sheet. It also causes the side to dome up. Now it's more stretching with the same dies.

The feeler gauge is often used to determine where the buck is resting against the metal, and where the metal needs to be stretched or shrunk in order to have more of the metal surface contact the buck. This is a long process in any case, because of the feisty nature of the 5052 the process is even slower than usual.

After lunch it's more of the same, stretch at the top front corner. Then check against the buck again, analyze with the feeler gauge and stretch the top rear corner with the small-radius stretching die on the planishing hammer.

By about an hour after our return from lunch you can see that the piece is really starting to come around. The top edge is down against the buck without the use of a clamp, the front corner is turned in tight and even the bottom rear corner and lower edge are wrapped around the buck.

The process continues as Fay shrinks and stretches. Stretching across the flattest part of the main panel with a fairly flat die in the Yoder. A test fit shows the fit to be pretty good but the piece has too much dome through the middle of the main panel. Fay stretches it top to bottom, then checks the fit again. All this stretching means the piece is growing bigger. As it fits the buck better the effect is much the same and Fay takes this opportunity to trim off the excess metal.

There is too much dome through the center, Fay stretches along the bottom edge with the linear stretching die, to take tension out of the lower lip and "let down" the center.

Fay often "encourages" the metal to take on the right form by bending it over the bench, "If the shape is honest the edge will form correctly, it will roll up right where we want it to."

In the case of the front lower edge, it's pulling away from the buck. Fay decides to do a small shrink and pull in the corner (note the photo sequence), the

Frequent test fits are all part of the shaping process, to see how far and where the shape is developing.

The paper pattern can also be put back on the piece as a way to double check the developing shape against the original.

Here Fay adds registration marks between the paper and the wheel fairing.

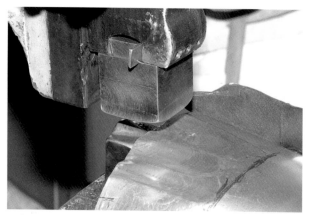

The thumbnail die creates a dome as the metal is inserted - and knocks it down as the piece is withdrawn, transferring energy through the area and making the metal thicker in the process.

Note the tunnel shape Fay uses as the piece goes back to the Yoder for more shrinking on the front corner.

Though he's known for power hammer work, Fay does use the wheel, to planish the rough areas and help create a soft crown through the center.

Fay is not afraid to occasionally do a little wrestling with the 5052.

At this point the fairing is coming around, though there's a lot of work yet to do, especially at the corners.

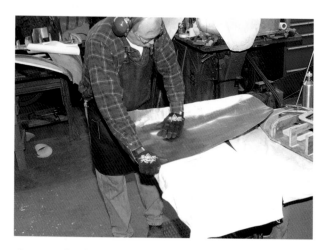

Laying the fairing flat, Fay uses his body to form up the side.

shrink is done gently with the small thumbnail dies on the Pullmax. After the shrink it's still a little too far from the buck so Fay forms it over the bench, explaining, "we did shrink it, and because of that when I bend it over it will want to suck up tight against the buck."

In the case of the back corner it isn't tight up against the buck, and we are dealing with a small lip so Fay shrinks it in the kick shrinker.

It still needs a little more shrinking, so Fay cold-shrinks it over a sand bag. Basically, by hitting it in a radiused area with a lot of strength, the force of the hammer blows causes the metal to shrink.

We're in pretty good shape now, though the panel still has a little too much shape, a little too much crown through the center. With a little more massaging, however, Fay minimizes the crown and excessive shape.

Victory is declared when the fairing sits on the buck with no clamps and follows the shape of the buck really well. When you hold the finished Fairing in your hands it's apparent that there is no tension in the piece. That is, it doesn't "oil can" when you hold it or twist it a little. With patience and skill Fay has created a "happy" piece of metal. One that holds its shape without clamps or undue tension.

FAY BUTLER INTERVIEW

The Fay Butler shop is in an old dairy barn turned metal shaping workshop. As you walk in the main door, past the wood-burning stove, you're likely to run into a partly assembled Pierce Arrow, one of Fay's personal projects. Farther back, buried under assorted this and that, is his other personal project, a rare Auburn Speedster.

To the left of the 'Arrow are the more pressing current projects. Like the Lotus seen a little farther along (now a finished and running car). In the next room are two huge power hammers. The real ones with the name Yoder cast into the frame (another sits outside awaiting restoration). Farther along is a Pullmax and at least one planishing hammer. And in the corner there's another smaller power hammer and a wheel and some other tools I probably missed. Hanging on the walls are bucks and sketches and sculpture of every possible description. Because Fay doesn't just build Lotus parts or Auburn parts or aircraft parts. Fay is one of those unique individuals who seem able to truly do 'whatever they set their mind to.' If he needs a new body section for a Pierce Arrow and the original was

Test fit number 669. It's come a long way - and still has a long way to go.

The corner is a little too tight, a situation that Fay remedies with a little stretching in the same area.

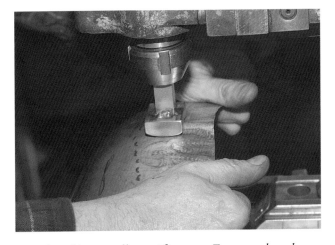

For shrinking small, specific areas Fay uses thumbnail dies in the Pullmax.

As the shape develops it becomes obvious the fairing is a little too big, so Fay marks the metal that will be trimmed off.

Now it's time to check the developing shape against the paper pattern.

When the metal is "shrunk" it still has to go some place. The caliper tells the tale, metal is thickest in the areas that received maximum shrinking.

cast aluminum, Fay will figure out a way to make a form and cast a piece of his own.

To understand how and why Fay does what he does you have to understand his philosophy of metal shaping, part of which is explained in this interview and part of which is explained in the text. To oversimplify his life's work, Fay has tried to elevate metal shaping from a black art to a scientific process. His emphasis is always on the underlying fundamentals so he and his students have a foundation for consistent metal shaping.

Fay, how did you get involved in this trade?

During a trip in college I went into a shop where they built car bodies from scratch. That fascinated me so much that after graduation I bugged the guy who owned the shop until he gave me a job. His name was Larry Amsley, from Chambersburg, Pennsylvania. Two years later I was on my feet back home in business for myself. Larry taught me how to see the shapes, we worked primarily with hand tools and air planishing hammers. Over the years I've expanded the equipment that I use to try to build larger panels of higher quality in less time.

Today I work for aircraft companies, Detroit prototype shops and private individuals, shaping parts and consulting. Once a month I put on an intense hands-on three-day seminar, for three individuals, designed for the serious amateur or professional. I'm also willing to help people with specific questions that arise while pursuing this trade. And I have some books available on specific metal working topics based on my 30 years of shaping. We are also bringing out a line of tooling and equipment.

Are there some people along the way who have helped you out or who you admire as shapers?

There are three people who have been significant influences: Scott Knight, Red Tweit and John Glover. They are outstanding human beings in addition to being spectacular craftsmen.

Fay, you like power tools and do very little hand shaping, can you give your reasons?

Hammering into a sand bag is a slow way to shape metal, you're using a one-sixteenth horsepower engine. I could make that wheel-fairing with hand tools but it would take 2 or 3 weeks and I would need a torch to anneal the material a number of times. I can make any part with a hammer and dolly and a tucking tool. With a torch, you can use heat to make the metal weaker so the little one-sixteenth horse engine has more effect. But in spite of the importance of the power tools it's the principles that are important. Ron Covell's classes are very good for entry level people and that's all hand tool work. There isn't anything you can't make with hand tools. I built a Mercedes body once with just hand tools.

There is some benefit to starting with hand tools and working with small pieces and then, as you understand the plastic flow of the material, you start hunting for more power. The power becomes a replacement for the one-sixteenth horsepower engine hammering into a sand bag.

If people do decide to buy power tools, what kind of progression should they follow, which tools should they buy first?

To start with you only need a little hand shrinker/stretcher, just buy the shrinking dies if you don't' want to spend any more than necessary. You also need a sand bag, pliers, and two body hammers, one high crown and one low crown. I avoid steel or fiberglass handles on my hammers because they're hard on your elbow.

Next you would want to buy a bench-top wheel, a bead roller and an air planishing hammer. The planishing hammer can be made out of the pistol grip air chisel everyone has in their tool box.

The next steps are really professional steps: You need a Pullmax style machine, that's about two thousand dollars used. You could actually get this at any point in the progression because it makes all hand beaters obsolete and now you can shrink with power.

And you need a power hammer, I've never seen a better source of energy. Cal Davis (see Sources) has a kit for two thousand dollars, or you could go to the high end and buy an original Yoder. Once you have the power hammer you can sell the bench-top wheel.

You differentiate form and shape, can you explain each one?

My twist on defining those concepts is that form is the folded component, shape is the change of thickness from shrinking and stretching. You can clamp form into a part, but you can't clamp shape. Compound curves are defined by the change in the material's thickness.

You said there are only three shapes in sheet metal, what are they?

High crown, low crown and reverses curve. Low crowns I stretch, high crowns I rough-in by shrinking and clean up by stretching - this wheel-fairing is a good example. A reverse curve is the reverse of a compound curve. Reverse in the way it's shaped and

Shrinking continues, this time on the lower rear corner.

With the basic shape determined it's time for a "skull session," to determine the best, most efficient, way to finish the fairing.

Using a sharp die, Fay begins massaging the fairing by stretching the back corner.

This is the die Fay used to stretch the back corner, chosen to match the radius of the very tight corner.

Here Fay is making notes on the outside of the fairing, indicating areas that need more stretching or shrinking.

Like a flexible feeler gauge, Fay uses strips of board to determine whether or not the piece is actually touching all the stations of the buck.

reverse in the way you make it, the way you affect the thickness change.

You talk a lot about the structure of metals and how the structure affects shaping?

Metals aren't molecules, they're crystals. Pure metals form very organized geometric patterns which are grains. The size of the grains can affect formability and mechanical properties. Whenever you are cold-working metals there are mechanisms in the grains that allow for slip to occur. When they are used up a strengthening mechanism known as work hardening or strain hardening occurs. The primary way of removing these strengthening mechanisms is with a time/temperature phenomenon known as annealing.

All metals are forgetful, where after annealing they go back to a softened or relaxed state, giving us back formability. If annealing is appropriately done after cold-working the net result is a smaller grain size which also increases formability.

Most people talk about shrinking or stretching period. You tend to differentiate each process depending on the tools and processes that are used?

All shrinking and stretching aren't the same. The processes are different, you are doing different things to the metal. For example, metals tend to work-harden less using thumbnail dies for shrinking, and steel dies for stretching. This becomes more apparent when working with higher strength heat-treatable aluminum and stainless steel, more difficult materials to shape.

What are your suggestions as to the best way to get started on a project?

You can build over the top of an existing part, or you can make a station buck. The important thing is to start with a paper pattern. The paper pattern lets you test ways of breaking the part up into various pieces depending on your skill level and tool selection. It's like getting a road map for the project. Now you can cut an accurate blank and have an idea of where the shape needs to occur.

In bigger projects where do you put the seams and why do you put them there?

I like seams placed where you can get to the back of the sheet to finish them. And the flatter surfaces give you larger die contact areas. I avoid putting seams on sharp edges because it is difficult to stretch them out after welding. With projects built from aluminum I tend to work with larger panels simply because aluminum is a more difficult material to weld as compared to steel.

The most difficult area to shape is the rear corner with its tight radius. Note that multiple clamps are needed to hold it on the buck at this time.

Fay marks the highlight line on the rear corner so he knows where to stop shrinking. "The shrink should never go deeper than the highlight line."

This linear stretching die is used...

Now it's time for more shrinking...

...to relieve tension along the top and back of the fairing.

...followed by a little stretching with the one-inch lower die.

Each test fit shows progress, part of which is measured by how many clamps are needed to hold the fairing to the buck.

Fay switches to the planishing hammer and a small-radius die to do a bit more stretching on the rear corner.

As the fairing conforms to the buck excess metal develops along the edges. Here Fay trims off some of that excess.

You have some specific ideas about welding, can you run through those and give some examples?

There are four factors that you have to understand when you weld: The chemistry of the puddle. Getting the right heat in the right spot. The shrinkage that will occur due to the temperature differential. The surface oxides and contaminants. Those four factors hold true today and they will hold true 2000 years from now. You have to address all four or you may not be making solid welds. For example:

Control of puddle - in steel you add filler rod to deal with trapped oxygen. When doing a single pass, butt-weld in mild steel use .035 inch wire, AWS class A 5.18, then sub group ER70s-6. With an alloy like 6061 aluminum, you need to add 30% filler material to eliminate solidification cracking.

Getting the right heat in right spot - this is a function of what you use. Be aware that oxy-acetylene heats through the air which is a poor conductor, giving a wider heat-affected zone than TIG. With TIG you need to use the appropriate sized tungsten on standard sheet metal. The standard recommendation is a .040 inch tungsten, good for 15 to 80 amps, DCEN.

You have to get over the fact that there's warpage and deal with it - just stretch the heat-affected-zone back out after welding.

Minimize surface oxides - you should clean the seam prior to welding and mechanically remove oxides which are always present. I like to wipe the area with clean rags and acetone in one direction just before I begin welding.

How do you feel about A-K steel?

A-K is what it is. It's a more formable product that's been better de-gassed, with a slightly lower carbon content and a finer grain. All of these are distinct advantages in shaping with two exceptions: dent resistance and cost. If you have limited power then more formability might be an advantage but not as much of an advantage as knowing what a compound curve is and how to get there. I prefer to use standard 19 gauge cold-rolled material because of cost and higher dent resistance. And of course I have the power to work that material, even multiple sheets at one time.

Any final comments?

No one was born with these skills, these are learned skills, you just need to start. You start with insufficient information and you problem-solve along the way. If you think something, some tool or process will work, then it probably will. Just get shaping.

Even with the many holes in the buck, it's hard to determine if the fairing is contacting all the stations or ribs, thus the flexible gauge.

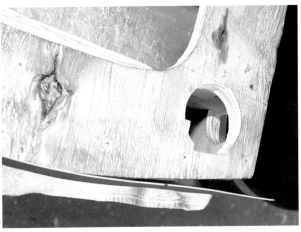

The fine tuning remains. Things like this front corner that refuses to pull in tight against the buck.

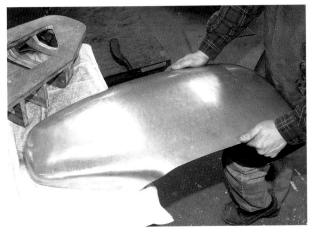

The piece is finally looking like half a wheel fairing, complete with a pretty good rear corner with its tight radius corner.

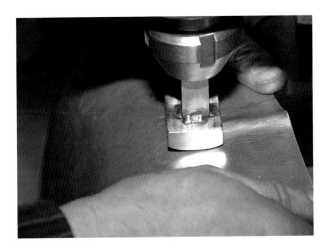

A condition that Fay remedies with a bit of discreet shrinking in the Pullmax along the front edge...

To eliminate some of the dome in the center of the piece Fay stretches along the lower part of the panel to relieve tension and minimize the crown.

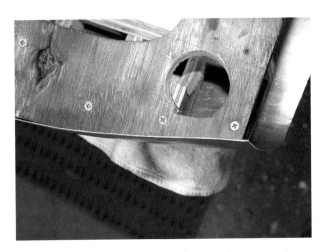

...which does in fact pull the lower edge up against the buck.

The top rear corner still isn't quite tight up against the buck. Fay uses a kick shrinker (an Erco 1447 from TCE) to shrink the lip of the upper corner.

Just a few final "adjustments" while the wheel fairing is on the buck...

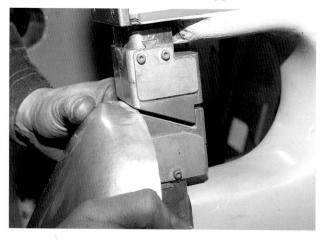

The close up shows the shrinking jaws on the Erco. This special set of jaws have the working surface tipped for better access.

...followed by further work on the planishing hammer.

Fay cold shrinks the same area even further by hammering the corner over a sand bag. The force of the blows is spread over the corner causing it to shrink.

Which leaves us with one half of a finished wheel fairing. One with no tension, no metal removal and true surfaces ready for polishing.

Fay Butler, Project Number Two

New Skin For An Old Lotus

Seen here is a major project from the shop of Fay Butler - the re-skinning of a 1955 Lotus race car. Being a real race car, the Lotus sheet metal had been repaired on more than one occasion. The car's current owner, Dave Belden, decided that rather than repair the repairs, he would simply replace the skin on the front of the car. In fact, he started off as one of Fay's students, but even after the intense seminar decided that the scope of the job were well beyond his abilities. Thus the Lotus took up residence in Fay's shop. What follows is a sequence, photographed by Fay with his trusty Leica, documenting the recreation of some very swoopy sheet metal, using the old sheet metal as the "buck."

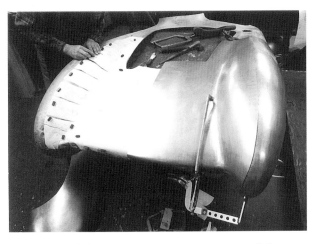

The start of the project: Paper patterning of the reverse curve on the inner panel. Note the other side is the finished (roughed out) fender.

The stretching occurs less inside the panel and progressively more toward the edge.

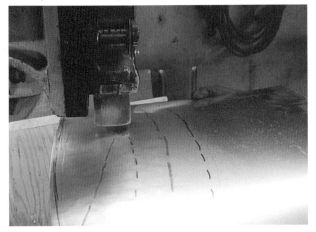

Work on the panel starts with shaping done using a linear stretch die. Lines show where the reverse curve starts.

Addition stretching is done close to edge of the panel.

Fay uses a ruler to determine where the reverse curve starts in front of driver in the cowl. The reverse curse starts right where the ruler lifts.

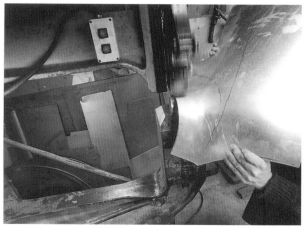

Stretching the reverse curve, from edge of sheet to the inside, is done with the linear stretch die. Note the line marking the beginning of the reverse curve.

More paper patterning, this time of the one-piece cowl and fender panel with a reverse curve.

Working from a different angle, Fay does further stretching of the reverse curve using the same die.

The paper pattern used here as a template.

At this point Fay has established the inside curve and is progressing with further stretching near the outside.

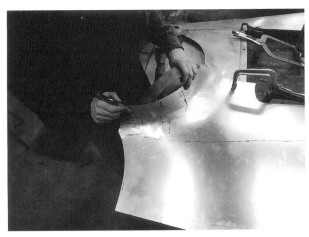

A progress check, done by laying the new panel over the original sheet metal and marking the areas that need more work.

You can see how the pattern has been transferred to the bare metal, the line indicates the beginning of the reverse curve.

Fay does the final stretching, or raising, of the very rear of the panel using the linear stretch die.

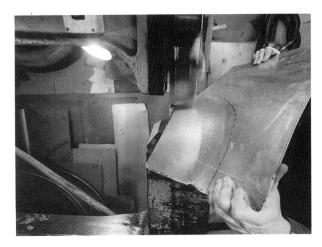

The linear stretch die is used again for stretching along this section of cowl.

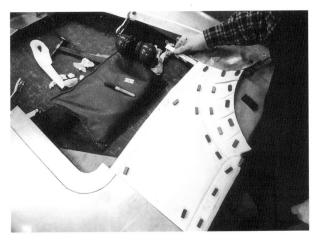

Here we have the fully developed paper pattern for the cowl with a line indicating where the reverse curve starts.

The finished cowl clamped in place with new side panels, prior to the detailing

Another paper pattern, for the lower front body panel. The panel supports the upper body so tougher 5052 aluminum is used instead of 3003.

The lower edge is turned using a rubber top die. This specialized die is used for special situations like this forming operation.

Shaping of the lower panel took patience due to the high tensile strength of the 5052 H34 material.

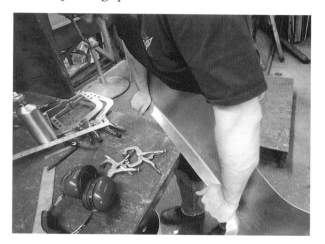

Once the turned edge is started the angle can be adjusted by simply pushing against a wooden bench.

Checking fit of new panel against the original is done by sliding a strip of poster board between the two pieces.

Now the piece needs further stretching of the area with the reverse curve.

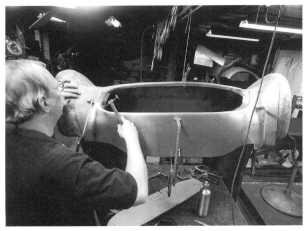

At this point the panel is nearly finished, Fay adds additional form with a body hammer.

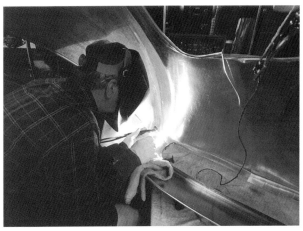

All the aluminum panels are welded with a Miller Aerowave TIG welder using a gas-purification system.

Here you see the finished lower panel ready for welding and detailing.

After grinding off the excess bead Fay finishes the seam with a planishing hammer.

The two panels are pin tacked together. The tape seen here on the back side of the weld is used to increase the quality of the weld by minimizing contamination by atmospheric gasses.

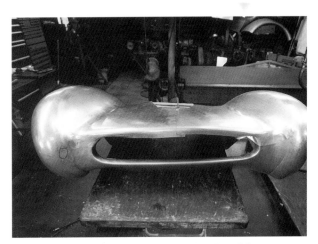

The finished front end prior to final welding. Note how the surfaces flow together at the seams.

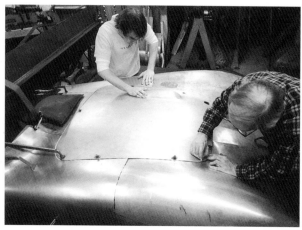

With help from Jonas Noble Fay uses the original hood to scribe guiding lines for the hood offset operation.

Turning the wire edge on an HD forming and flanging machine manufactured by TCE Corporation.

Using the Pullmax with an offset die, Fay creates a recess for the hood.

Close up shows the first operation, turning a 90 degree flange with the appropriate tooling to create the right radius for 3/16inch edge wire.

Here the edge of the panel is determined with a paper pattern and automotive body sweeps (which provide increased accuracy).

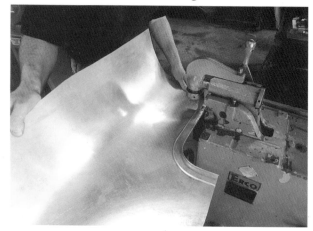

Overview showing the second of three edge-wire operations.

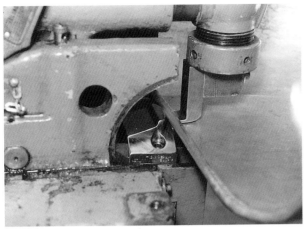

Close up shows special tooling designed and manu-factured by Fay for this application.

Fay grinds off excess bulk from the weld bead.

Close up detail of wire edge and hood offset.

A hand-held planishing hammer is used to stretch out shrinkage that occurred in the heat affected zone.

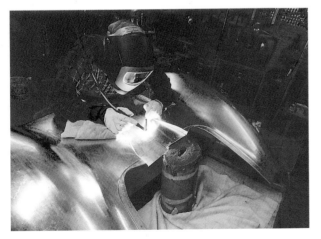

The pieces are pin-tacked together prior to the final welding.

The finished project, an old race car with a com-plete new nose - and the original sheet that can be used for vintage racing.

Chapter Four - Rob Roehl

Tanked In Minneapolis

A Signature Donnie Smith Gas Tank

For the bikers in the crowd we bring you Rob Roehl, sheet metal fabricator for well-known custom bike builder Donnie Smith. Rob's task is to build a gas tank from scratch, no small job considering the extreme amount of shape in the typical

motorcycle tank. Though he sometimes works free-hand, Rob decided to make a rather elaborate buck for this job, "so we could reproduce this shape exactly and offer it as a signature Donnie Smith tank."

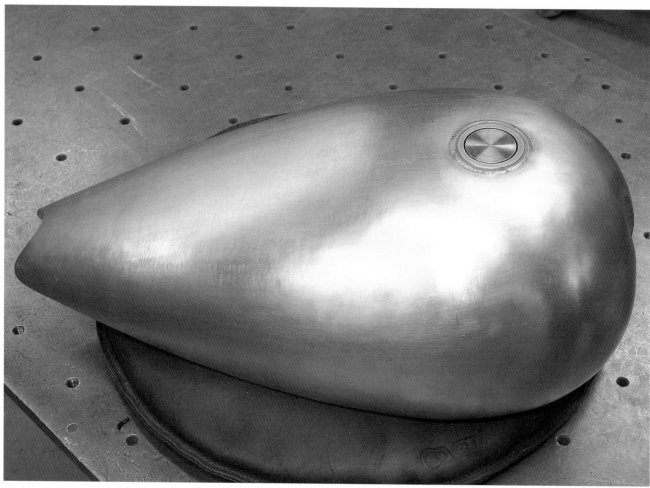

When looking at a complex shape like this, complete with tunnel and gas tank, it's truly hard to believe the whole thing started out as one sheet of cold-rolled steel.

Rob starts with a drawing. "I try to put on paper what's in my mind's eye. You have to measure the backbone first of course. Usually I try several different renderings until I find something that I like and then I hold it up against the frame to see if I like it."

"Then once I have a side view, I have to figure out what the top view should look like. I know what the length is, I use that dimension and sketch a top view that I like and cut that out. I do everything in halves, with a mirror image. That way they're the same right to left. And then I put them together to make sure they line up. I also have to figure out where I want the top of tunnel."

Once he has renderings that he likes Rob can start building the buck. The actual templates are cut from 1/2 inch, MDF (medium density fiberboard) on the band saw. After cutting, the various pieces are clamped together. Rob puts the first part of the buck on top of the top view cut outs and makes a new cut out that represents the top view of one side, from the edge of the MDF out (check photos to relieve confusion).

Now he screws the new side pieces to the main stem of the buck. "You do have to pre-drill the MDF before forcing a screw into it," explains Rob, "or the material will split." He marks the outside of the stem of the buck with a centerline and then drills the holes for the coarse sheet rock screws and bolts it all back together again.

Time now for some Jiffy Foam (Rob already had the profile that he wanted, so didn't make a whole tank from foam). He puts Jiffy on the buck and glues it together with Elmer's glue, He marks the foam with a marks-a-lot, trims it on the band saw and places it on the buck. Then it's time to trace again and cut again.

For roughing in the shape of the foam Rob uses a cheese grater. "After I have it roughed in," explains Rob, "I switch to a sanding block and some 80 grit paper." The process is repeated for each top quarter. "I didn't find it necessary to glue it to the wooden part of the buck," says Rob, who goes on to explain, "it's a good idea to sand a little, set it on the bike and then step back to check the shape." You could carve both sides, but I'm going

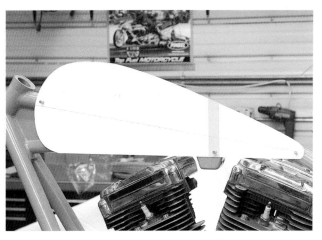

After making a drawing of the tank, Rob makes a side view and tries it on the bike for size.

The top view is next - actually made up of two halves, or mirror images.

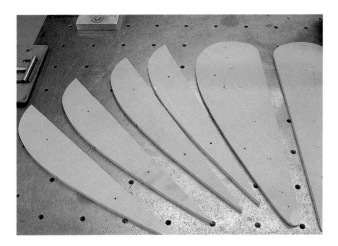

Once Rob has the outline he likes and knows the height of the tunnel he can cut out the parts of the buck from MDF.

The various parts are now assembled into the back-bone for the buck...

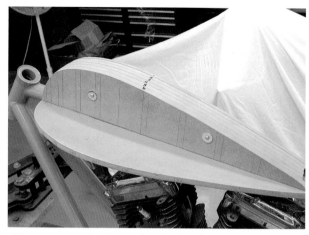

Here you see the basis for the buck.

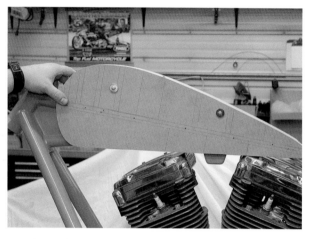

...which drops over the top tube thus.

Foam is marked before being...

The top-view profile is next. All the pieces are held together with sheet rock screws.

... cut out on the band-saw.

to just do one side and make mirror images for the other side."

"Then I studied where I want my stations and marked that on the wood." When it comes time to determine how many stations to use, Rob suggests putting more stations where there is more shape. "Out at the tail I have three or four inches between each one, up front where I'm in the middle of the compound curve I've got them much closer together. I'm going to put little solid pieces of MDF on either end."

Thin slices of foam are cut out wherever Rob wants a station, and used as a template to mark the outline on another piece of MDF. In this way each of the very accurate stations are fabricated.

"I traced them generous and I cut them generous," says Rob. "Then I made solid pieces for the ends, cut them and sanded everything with 80 grit by hand.

PATTERN MAKING

The buck is finished, assembled with Elmer's glue and sheet rock screws, all holes are pre-drilled. Rob went over it with 80 grit on a sanding block to even up all the edges, and also used a straight edge to ensure that the bottom stayed flat per the design. "The buck can be as elaborate as you want," says Rob. "In hindsight, I probably didn't need this many stations."

Before making the patterns and eventually the sheets of steel Rob needs to decide how many pieces to use to make the tank and where the seams should be placed. "What's left in terms of pattern making is theory and ability. For a beginner," explains Rob, "it might make sense to fabricate the side piece out of 2 or 4 pieces."

"My deal is I like to put a seam where I can work it out later, I try not to put the seam where I can't get a hammer and dolly in later. Otherwise you can't go in and metal finish it later. And I try to put a seam on what I call a natural curve. I'm probably going to split the side about half way up," says Rob. "So I don't have to put all that shape in one panel. And of course because this has a flat bottom, the bottom will be a separate piece."

For the patterns, Rob likes to use butcher paper or poster board. Rob likes a pretty loose pat-

By using the foam, shaped with a cheese grate, Rob will be able to create...

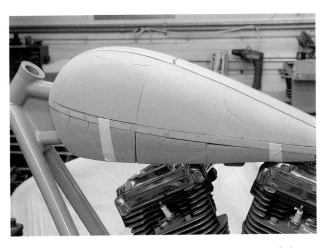

...a full size three dimensional representation of the gas tank. This is allows him to actually see the tank before starting on the metal work.

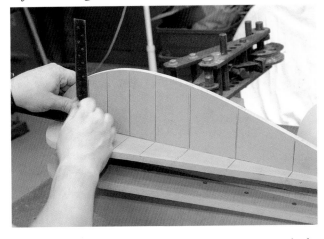

Next the locations of the various stations are marked on the backbone.

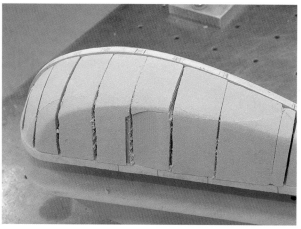

The foam is placed back on the buck and cut at the point of each station.

Time now to mark where the seams will be placed.

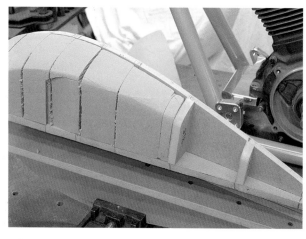

Slices of the foam are used as patterns, which are then used to cut out the stations from MDF.

Light poster board is pinned to the buck and used to make the paper pattern...

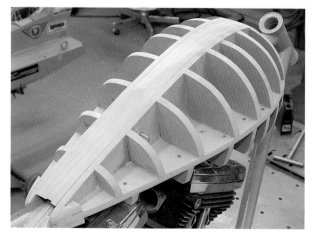

The completed buck positioned on the bike's top tube.

...which must be cut wherever there's going to be a seam.

tern, "I find that it's easier to make the part oversize and trim to fit the buck than to make a real precise pattern and piece. Now I mark where the seam is going to be, I always leave the bottom open 'till last."

Rob uses thumb tacks to stick the board to the buck and marks the bottom of the pattern from the back side, "I leave an extra 1/2 inch." Rob cuts the pattern, then slits the bottom and uses tape and push pins to attach the pattern to the buck. With the bottom done, Rob starts on the top. Trimming poster board at the line he drew earlier that represents the seam.

Now Rob marks the edge of the pattern where it needs to be trimmed, "where there's too much material," and takes the pattern off the buck.

"I transfer the outline to another piece of paper, that way I can use a straight edge on the bottom and add a little extra material on the lower front corner, because I know that area needs so much shrinking that it's nice to have some extra material there. I make the slots so I know where I'm going to have to do most of my shrinking."

"I leave the pattern a good 1/2 to 3/4 inch too big on the edges, more where I have to do a lot of shrinking. I've done it where I cut the pattern and the metal really tight, and it only got me into trouble. Ron Covell teaches you to cut the pattern and the piece a little big, then lay the two pieces on the buck, they will overlap, and you can scribe the line and trim it for a perfect fit."

"You could do this with just stretching and a little edge shrinker, but that would be hard. I do it half and half, stretch the center and then shrink the edges. That way you don't work one part of the tank too much."

Now we will make a pattern for the top. "I do everything in halves," adds Rob. "The mirror image thing. So I only cut the top pattern to go from the seam on the side to the centerline on the top of the buck. I'm going to be pretty generous though and give myself about a 1/2 inch overlap. Then I cut slots where it will shrink but there's so little shape in the top that you really wouldn't have to."

Slits are cut in the areas where the shrinking will take place. The degree of overlap indicates the relative degree of shrinking necessary.

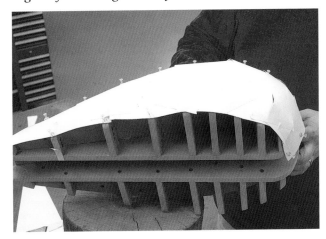

Here's the finished paper pattern pinned to the buck.

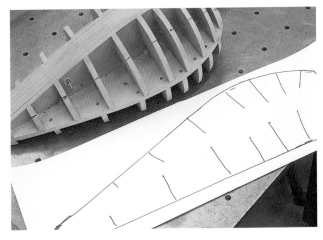

Rob goes one step farther, and transfers the outline of the pattern to a second piece of paper. This second pattern is the one he uses to mark the metal.

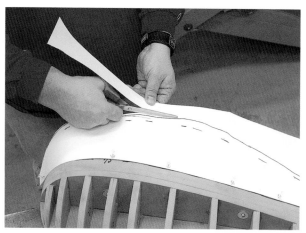

The second pattern is pinned to the buck and cut out along the seams.

Thumbnail shrinking dies are the work of Loren Richards...

The metal is cut a little bigger than the pattern, to ensure there's enough material to overlap the adjoining sheets.

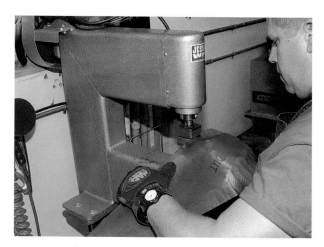

...the same man who designed and built this very nice, small power hammer.

Topographical map drawn on the tank indicates high and low areas.

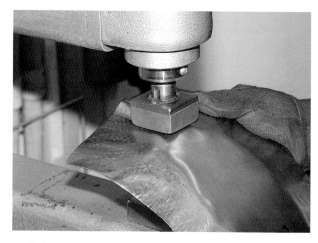

Rob begins the actual metal work by shrinking his way around the perimeter of the panel.

"Put the templates on the sheet metal and cut. Cut the steel with anything that works for you. The tank is made from 18 gauge (.045 inch) 1010, aluminum-killed steel. The bottom will be 14 gauge. That's where we cut in the mounts and where the weight is supported so it helps if it's a heavier piece of steel, and you're not doing much shaping to that piece either."

"I position the side panel over the buck and then figure out where I'm going to have to do the most work. In the front we will have to shrink, the edge at the middle and back will be more of a roll. Then I will have to stretch the center as marked. Basically, I've interpreted where the shape needs to go. I will start by shrinking the edge at the front, then switch tooling to stretching dies and work on the center."

START SHAPING
Tool of Choice
I've learned to keep my tooling and material clean. I don't use lube on steel, I use it on aluminum. Loren Richards made the hammer, it's like a mini Pullmax. Same idea, a simple reciprocating machine with a heavy frame and tooling holder."

Rob starts on the marked front edges of the metal, working across the surface. In only five minutes or less he stops and takes it out for the first check against the buck (note the photos). Obviously the piece needs more shape so Rob goes back to the machine and continues to work the same area. Time for another test fit. Then he hammers the edges where there's a shoulder at the edge of the shrinking area, this will make it easier to stretch the material on the small power hammer, with no edge for it catch on.

Now he changes the tooling, (note the tooling pictures.) "Loren makes these thumbnail shrinking dies from high grade steel," explains Rob, then has them hardened."

At this point Rob is starting to put more shape into the whole panel. The stretching dies move the metal fast, in only a couple of minutes the waffles are eliminated and the center is starting to stretch up.

After the first two rounds of shrinking the areas that require shrinking are coming along just fine...

...but the area in the center of the panel needs to be stretched...

...which Rob accomplishes with a nice sturdy wooden mallet.

For stretching on the small power hammer Rob uses a Duralon upper die and crowned lower die.

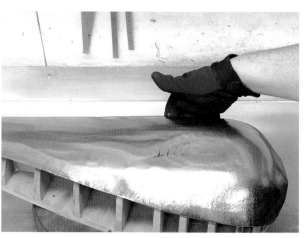

Time for a test fit, the piece is moving along quickly, but this is only the first panel.

The stretching dies are used to raise the center of the panel...

To get the sides to come down closer to the buck Rob continues to raise the panel through the center.

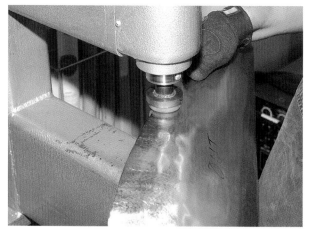

... and eliminate most of the waffles left from the shrinking operations.

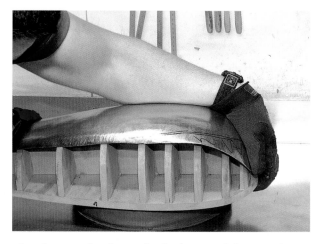

Another test fit shows the bottom and front to be too far away from the buck.

After the stretching sequence, Rob changes tools to, "do a little more shrinking around the front to pull the front edge down to the buck more. To concentrate the shrinking at the front so it gathers and will curl the metal." Note the close up photos of the side and how it doesn't come down far enough on the buck.

"Because we've already got some shape in the metal, the shrinking will curl the whole thing," explains Rob. "The effect won't be just along the edge. Something else I do, I put the piece on the buck and press down on it, and when I get a pucker at one of the corners, that's where I've got to do more shrinking, that's where there's too much metal."

A test fit confirms a much better fit at the front of the buck than farther back. "Now I'm going to shrink that next area to get the tail to come down more on the buck," explains Rob. As predicted, the next test fit shows that the tail has come down onto the buck quite a bit.

At this point Rob does some stretching with the world's oldest tool, all through the center and well into the tail. Then more test fitting. "My whole goal right now is just to get the basic shape," says Rob, "to get the steel to relate better to the buck."

Rob spreads the tank side a little by hand and does a test fit again, Now Rob decides to, "raise the center because that will bring down the front edges. I've done as much shrinking as I'm comfortable doing so I will raise the center which will in effect bring down the edges. Note the photo of the 'contour map' on the tank side where stretching will take place.

"As I stretch it with the hammer I get puckers along the edge, which tells me I've got too much metal there, you can shrink that area later or whatever works." Now Rob stretches out the waffles and walnuts put in the lower edge by the hammer action. The lower part of the front corner still needs to come down.

"It's a little too tight at this point," explains Rob, "the radius right through the middle, so I will hammer the edges there and open up the middle, and that should bring down the front edges."

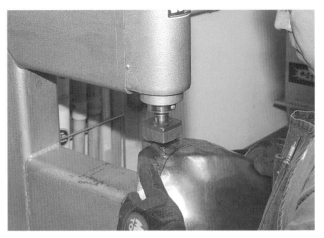

To bring those areas tighter in against the buck Rob installs the shrinking dies again and goes over the front...

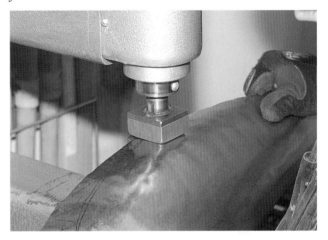

...and the bottom of the side panel.

Not perfect but a better fit than the last time.

Who says violence never accomplished anything. In this case it accomplished a lot or stretching.

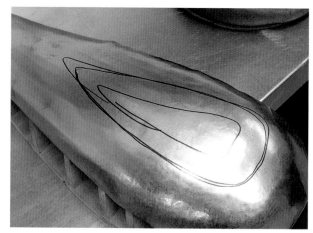

The panel needs still more stretching through the center, as notes by the "map" on seen here.

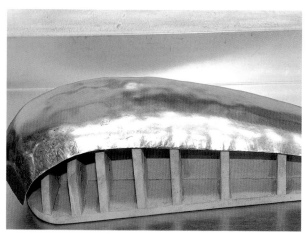

Though the resulting surface is a little rough.

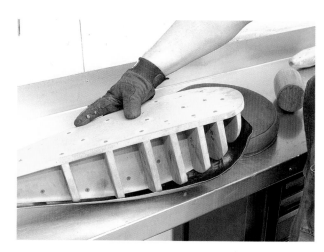

And the fact that the front and bottom are still too far away from the buck.

A problem Rob can deal with through careful use of the soft Duralon die.

Rob stretches the panel from front to back with his wooden mallet.

Time now for another test fit, followed by more hammer work and another check against the buck. "It gets harder at the end," notes Rob.

Rob does some thinking at this point, pushes the metal down against the buck to see where it buckles, where it fits and where it doesn't. The metal does buckles (note the mark) when Rob pushes it down against the buck, so Rob shrinks it there with the small hand shrinker.

The next test fit documents just how much better the overall shape conforms to the buck, than it did just a few test fits ago. How both the nose and tail have tucked in.

Rob does a little more shrinking at the edge with the hand shrinker, then another test fit, then a bit more hammer work. "Now it's time to use the wheel to slowly raise the center a bit more, the key word being slowly. My heavy rough work is done, I'm 60% of the way there, now I can use the wheel to smooth out some of the lumps and to slowly finish creating the shape. I start out with real low pressure on the metal and run over the tops of my lumps. The idea is to slowly work them up and smooth 'em out."

Now Rob installs a flatter wheel and rolls the panel the short way, "It will work on my curl a little bit and eliminate more of the lumps. Again these are real light passes, I'm trying to smooth more than shape right now."

"From here on it's mostly wheel work," explains Rob. "I use the hammer for the rough-in part of the work." There is a little sag along the lower edge toward the rear, which Rob takes out with a dolly and a slap hammer. At this point the bottom edge fits the buck, but the top edge at the middle rear is still raised up off the buck, so it's more slap hammer work, "What I'm doing is slapping that edge down."

Now it's back on the wheel. We've been at it less than two hours at this point. Next he rolls the edge with the slap hammer on the T-dolly with the crowned head.

At this point the edges meet the buck pretty well, note the test fit photos. Then it's back to the wheel, rolling both the long and the short way in the middle of the side panel. "I'm trying to raise

Now Rob does a test fit and squeezes the tank side on the buck, the bowed out section you see means there's too much metal there.

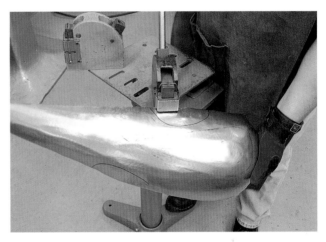

Which Rob addresses by shrinking along the edge with the small hand shrinker.

Which is likewise used at the front of the panel.

A test fit shows how the edges have in fact come down closer to the buck as a result of the shaping.

...the wheel in turn eliminates the lumps left by the hammer and raises the metal still further.

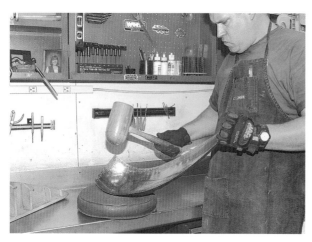

To raise the panel through the center, Rob uses the wooden hammer...

The effects are subtle and hard to judge from this angle, but the stretching has raised the center which brings the edges down.

followed by a session on the wheel with a fairly flat lower wheel...

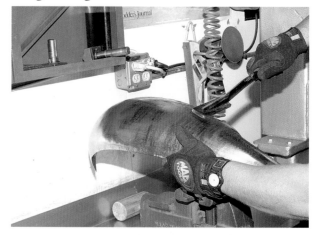

A small low spot is eliminated with the slap hammer and dolly.

the very center part," says Rob. "I've got more pressure on the wheel and I'm being more aggressive." Sometimes Rob gets a twist in the panel, "because I'm working one area more than another," and he has to twist it back into shape.

"Most metal shapers don't do this, but I like to scuff the metal with a scotchbrite pad, to get rid of all the track marks. Now I can tell more easily where I've been.

After forming the other side of the tank, and the center panel (not shown) Rob is ready to trim and weld the three panels into the top of the new gas tank.

With the buck on its side, "so I can see both the top and bottom" and holding the side panel in position with his free hand, Rob scribes a line where the two panels meet along with a couple of witness marks. The process is repeated for the other side then all the panels are taken off the buck.

As Rob explains, "I decided it was easier to trim the top panel because it has less shape. The actual trimming is done with a Wiss tin snips, as you can imagine, I'm a big proponent of sharp tin snips. If you catch them on sale they're only about twelve bucks each."

Rob goes on to explain, "I usually cut in two steps, first I cut up to about 1/8th inch from the line I scribed. Then I go back and cut right at the line. Sometimes I use a power nibbler or some kind of power tool for the first cut. But for the final cut I always use a tin snips, it gives you a real accurate clean cut and it's easy to control. Cutting with the snips might take you a little while but it doesn't distort the edge. It does leave a little burr on the edge and I will knock that off with the belt sander. I leave the end of the panel a little long and will trim that later. When the trimming is finished I can pin the panel back onto the buck and check my fit."

"When it's overlapped, like when you scribe the line, it won't fit perfect," says Rob, "so now I look at it to see if there's someplace I should trim before I start tack welding. In this case I have to trim a little bit at the back of the panel. This is one of the most critical part of the fabrication, the

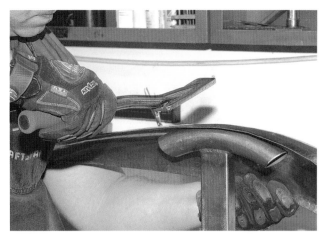

The slap hammer and a post dolly are used at this point to get the edge to roll down even more...

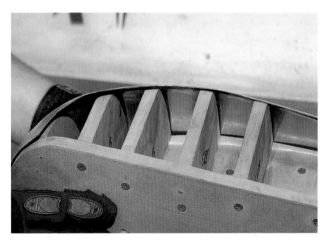

...as seen here in this test fit.

To raise the center still more Rob uses the wheel, working the short way.

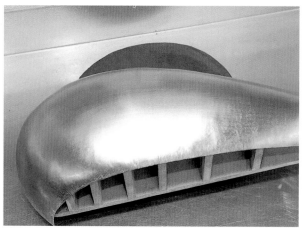

Near the end of the project Rob scuffs the panel so he can more easily trace any additional work.

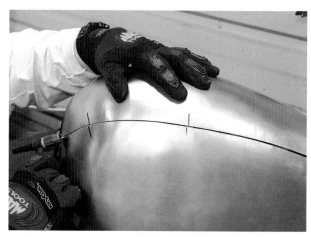

After trimming along the scribed line the tack welding can begin.

Here we have the three panels prior to assembly.

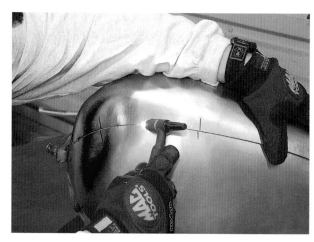

These are small fusion welds, done one at at time...

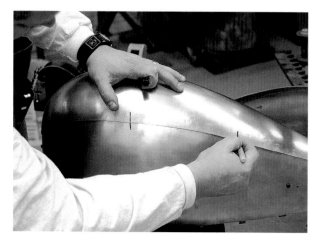

With the center panel screwed to the buck, Rob fits the right side panel and then makes two witness marks.

...with hammer and dolly work as needed before proceeding down the seam.

better the fit is the easier it is to weld, you don't have to weld it and then beat the piss out of it trying to get it flat. I'd rather have a little gap than an overlap. Once there's an overlap you've got double the metal so it's really hard to work that seam later."

Rob declares that the right side is OK, "I've got my lows and highs but we can work that out later. On the left side of the tank there's a mismatch between the two panels at the back. I think I will tack the two and then work the one up and the other down and get them to come around that way."

"I always start at one end and work toward the other," explains Rob. "Here I'm starting at the front where the two pieces have a real good relationship, then I work toward the rear."

Rob starts tack welding the right side panel to the top panel with the heli-arc welder, doing small fusion-welds without any filler rod. Each tack is examined before going on to the next. Rob stops often to knock down the metal after a tack, or to use a putty knife to avoid having one piece overlap another. The two pieces don't just fall together, Rob does a tack or two, examines that area and the area downstream, then knocks down any areas that are going high, pushes and pulls the outer side panel into achieve good fitment with the top panel, and then does another tack. A pucker develops part way down the seam, causing Rob to comment, "I will have to shrink that later when the tank is off the buck."

Because of the gap Rob goes to the far end, and tacks the two panels together there. Before tack welding the center of the seam the metal on either side is slapped down to minimize the gap, then the tack welding can continue.

Note: the photo sequence focuses on the tack welding of the right-side seam.

THE LEFT SIDE.

Again, Rob starts at the front, tacking, adjusting and working his way down the seam. If there's a little gap then he uses some rod, for fusion welds the two pieces have to be touching pretty good.

Close up shows how Rob holds the seam tightly together while doing each fusion weld.

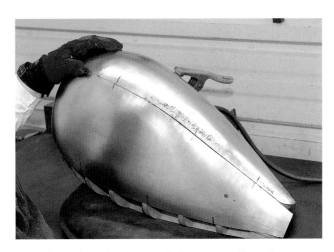

On the right side the panels line up well at the top and bottom of the seam, but the gap is pretty wide in the middle.

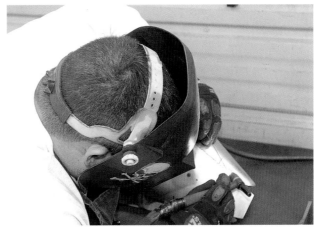

Rob goes ahead and welds the area at the back of the tank, using filler rod to make a good strong tack weld.

At the front of the tank too, Rob does a few strong tack welds, using filler rod for each one.

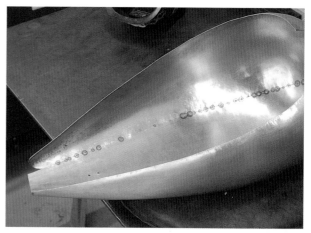

Here we see the tank after all three panels are tack welded together. The beauty of this situation is the fact that the seam can be accessed from either side.

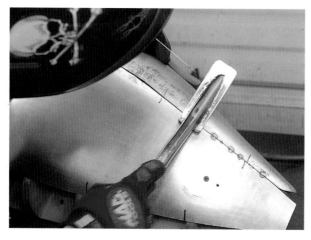

Now the slap hammer can be used to knock down the metal along the middle of the seam, effectively bringing the two edges closer together.

The post-dolly is mounted in the vise prior to...

Finally, the center of the seam can be tack welded together.

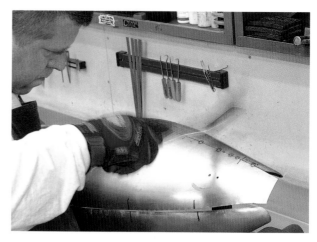

...a little work with the slap hammer.

Now Rob takes the tank off the buck, before it's too late.

Once off the buck it's time for a little slapping and adjusting to both seams, then more tack welding on the left side. Rob does a number of mini sequences, flipping the tank over, working the two lips on the right side so they're even, then flipping the tank to do another couple of tacks.

On the left rear, Rob trims metal from the back corner, then the two sides really come together. Now he does a series of tack welds on the tail end of the left-side seam.

"Now I look at where my problem areas are," says Rob. "If you can't see them you can feel them. You can pick up a lot of problems with your hand that you won't see with your eye."

On the right side Rob knocks down the pucker. Then he moves along both seams adjusting the areas up or down. It doesn't take very long to get the seams ready for welding Rob does both on and off-dolly work on the seam, depending on whether he's trying to raise a low spot or knock down a high spot.

"I don't worry too much about it getting lumpy, because the welding will make it lumpy too. With the slapper on the outside and the broad face of the dolly underneath, it's easy to raise the seam, the dolly acts as the hammer pounding against the seam from the bottom." Rob also does some hammer work with the wooden mallet, on the seam from the bottom.

"Sometimes an overlap develops, just because or sometimes as a result of trying to weld too fast. And then I just get the cut-off tool with the thin wheel and cut a seam and start over with the tack welds. Or you get a twist in the tank, in fact this one has a little twist, Usually you can armstrong it back until it's straight. If it's too bad you have to go back and figure out what you did that caused the twist."

The welding is done at 75 or 80 amps, with a .045 inch 70 S2 welding rod and a standard tip. "I used to use 100 to 110 amps," notes Rob, "but now I'm comfortable welding at lower amperage levels and I get less warpage." Rob does the right

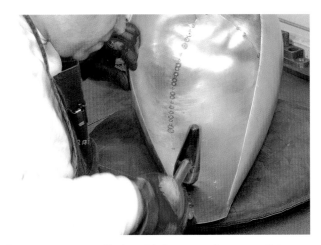

Low spots are really just high spots when seen from the other side.

The tools used to finish the seam before final welding are the familiar hammers and a dolly with a radius that matches the inside of the tank.

With patience Rob creates a near-perfect seam before staring on the final welding.

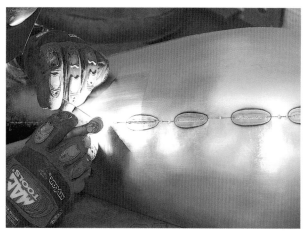

Final welding is done in "stitches" moving form front to rear.

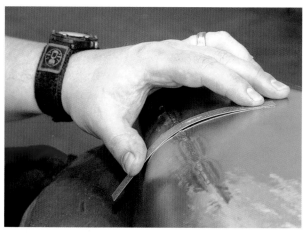

Here's a piece of seam "before" any metal finishing.

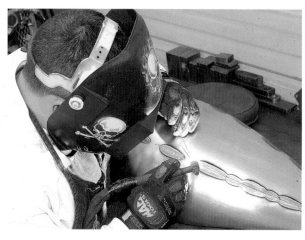

When he gets to the end, he switches to the other side, then comes back later to fill in the gap in the first seam.

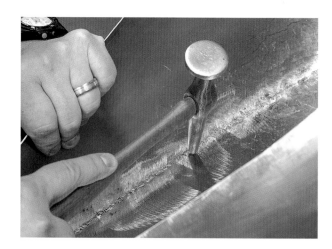

First, Rob raises an obvious low spot.

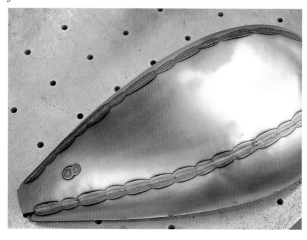

Working in this patient way, Rob finish welds the two top seams with very little warpage.

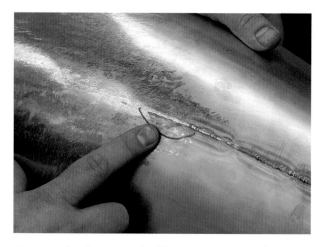

Despite the first round of hammer work, a low area remains.

side first, welding one inch sections, starting at the front and going toward the rear.

After allowing the stitch welds to cool, Rob goes back and welds up the gaps, creating one continuous seam on both sides. "Sometimes you get puckers as you weld the seam, and you have to go back and knock down a spot before you go on, but this one went real well. The key to a good seam is having the parts fit well in the first place."

If you ask Rob how fast to weld a seam on a steel tank, he says it's up to the person doing the welding, "You can weld as fast as you're comfortable, it all depends on your skill level. If you go too fast you can wreck a lot of stuff though."

FROM SHAPING TO METAL FINISHING.

"Prior to any filing I want to get the seam flat with the hammer and dolly. The idea of the filing is more to remove the very high spots, you don't really want to grind down the weld, you want to planish it with a hammer and dolly, not grind away the weld.

"I use a Vixen file, preferably a sharp one. It will also show up any remaining low spots. It acts like the guide coat that a body man uses to find high and low spots. I work out all the top seams and the top itself while I can, before the bottom goes in."

Note the sequence on the low spot. The way Rob raises a low spot with the pick end of his hammer, before switching to the hammer and dolly, then back to the file to check the progress. The dolly work is done "off dolly" with the narrow radius of the dolly up against the seam and Rob hammering not just the seam but the metal on either side so the dolly raises the low spot.

"I use light pressure on the file. I adjust the surface while I'm doing this, I find other little low or high spots and adjust those too. It's hard to realize just how important this finish work is. This level of finishing is the real key if you are going to do any polishing or plating later.

"As I get close to finished on that area I start to fan out with the file so I see how that area relates to the areas around it. I'm using almost no pressure, just the weight of the file on the metal."

You can't do all the "finishing" with the file or you risk removing too much metal.

Once the area is mostly flat, Rob hits it with the Vixen file.

A survey shows only a few small lingering high and low spots.

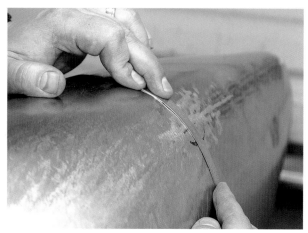

A progress check shows the surfaces in pretty good alignment though it can always be better.

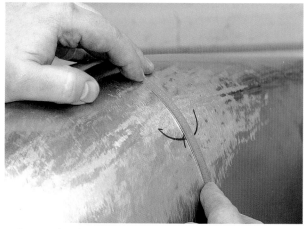

The result of all the patient filing, and hammer and dolly work, is a very nice contour (Rob re-marked the original low spot).

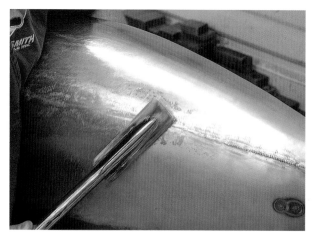

Now Rob goes over the area again with the slap hammer and dolly, carefully adjusting the surfaces up and down.

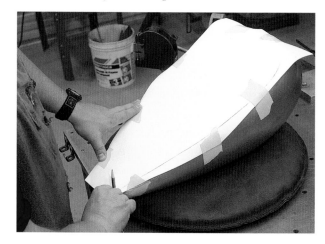

The bottom panels and tunnel are next. The first step is the manufacture of another paper pattern.

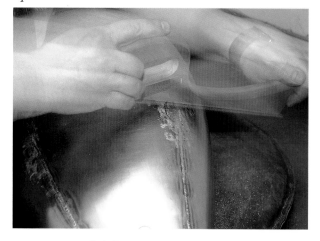

Hammer and dolly work is followed by more light filing with the Vixen file, working an area bigger than the spot we're trying to finish.

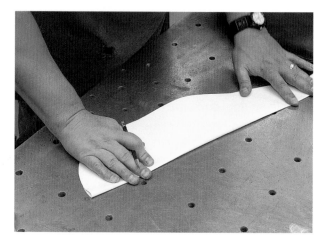

Once he has a pattern, Rob folds it to make sure it's symmetrical...

Rob files the area one or two inches away from the low and finds that the spot is not only nearly finished but that it relates well to the areas nearby. "It's important to feather the area out as you file," adds Rob.

INSTALL THE BOTTOM

Rob starts the installation of the bottom panels by taping on a piece of paper that will act as a template. After taping it on tight Rob rubs the edge with a pencil as shown, explaining, "This is the most accurate way I've found to mark the edge."

After marking the edge and removing it from the tank, Rob cuts it out carefully then folds it and marks the centerline. "The tunnel will be two inches wide so I mark that line one inch on either side of the centerline. Then I like to do a flange, so I make another line 3/8 inch on the inside of the two lines that mark the edge of the tunnel."

"I have to make room for the top of the tube where it meets the two tubes coming from the oil tank area. This is kind of an eyeball deal. But if it's too tight you can always go back and open it up."

Note the photos of cut out pieces of metal, the bottom panels cut from 14 gauge steel, "for durability," with a flange formed on the brake.

During the test fit Rob repeats the comment made earlier, "My goal is to not have any overlap, between the two pieces of steel."

...and so he knows where to mark the centerline.

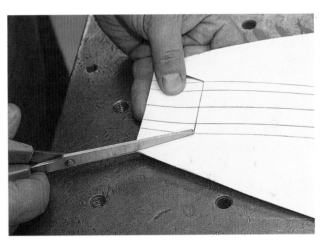

The pattern is marked with a second set of lines that mark the flange, and another set of lines that marks out the flare at the back of the tank.

Here you can see the one bottom panel, with the matching paper pattern. Note the flange on the inside lip.

After he's sure the panel fits, Rob uses magnets to hold it in place...

Rob armstrongs the panel, which is 14 gauge for durability and because it supports the weight of the tank.

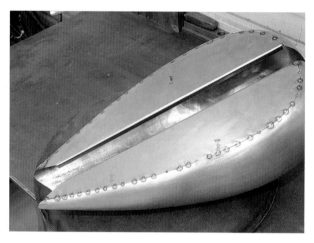

...and tack welds both panels to the bottom of the tank.

A slapper is used to get it to conform better to the OD of the pipe.

A pipe of just the right diameter (1/4 inch smaller than the actual tunnel) is used to form the tunnel.

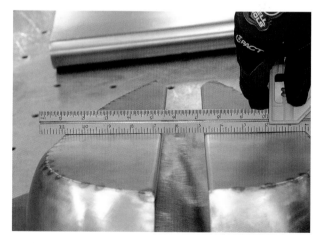

Before inserting the tunnel Rob makes sure the two bottom panels are level and flat.

The first half of the bottom is put in place with a series of small fusion welds "I start at the front of the tunnel and pull the metal together as I move toward the back of the tank. Then I hammer and dolly the seam so everything fits real nice."

Now Rob does a series of tack welds using filler rod, spaced less than an inch apart, working from the front to the rear again. "Then I go over the seam with the hammer and dolly. I like to roll the edges a little bit so they don't 'tepee' so much where they meet, you get a much nicer seam that way." Rob follows the same procedure for the other side.

FORMING THE TUNNEL.

Rob formed the tunnel in a separate operation. The design calls for a tunnel two inches wide. As Rob explains, "I use a 1 3/4 inch tube for the brake, to form the tunnel. I want a 2 inch tube, but there's some spring-back, so I use a tube that's a quarter inch smaller. This is length that I want. I made it so when I get it folded I will still have too much metal and then I can trim it to fit."

Rob mounts the tube on the surface table with machinist-grade clamps, but is quick to explain, "You could just do this with a tube and two C-clamps, you just need to be sure it's clamped down there pretty good. I do try to bend it as evenly as I can, then I take my slapper and get it tight against the pipe."

"The bottom needs to be really flat before I mark my trim lines on the tunnel, so I use a rule to check it and bend the panels a little if I need to. Then I just mark it with the Mark's-a-lot, nothing too fancy."

The trimming is done with a small power shears. " I kind of sneak up on the line, don't take too big a bite all at once."

Rob explains that the flange on the two bottom pieces adds strength to that seam and makes the welding easier. "When I do the bottom pieces without the flange, then the metal wants to drop when I start welding. There's a lot of tension in that bottom and when you hit it with heat then it just wants to fall. This is my way to avoid that."

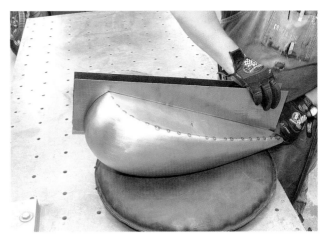

The raw tunnel should fit snug between the two bottom pieces.

So Rob can mark the outline...

...and cut the tunnel to size.

Rob checks the tunnel for fit.

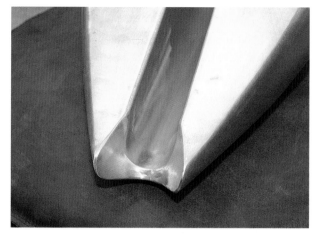

Close up shows the nice flare at the back where the top tube meets the other two tubes.

Then starts the tack welding process.

The mounts are part of a sophisticated mounting system developed at Donnie's shop. Both halves of each mount are cut, milled and fabed in-house.

Which is followed by final welding and finish work.

The tunnel is 1/4 inch wider than the diameter of the top tube. Rubber cushions are used to prevent any contact between tunnel and tube.

As for fitting the tank on the bike, Rob explains, "I like about 1/8th inch between the tank and the tube. Some space in case the tank rocks a little. Sometimes we use battery cushion material or hard rubber, it depends on the application to act as a cushion and help prevent any metal-to-metal contact.

Rob had the position on the top tube figured out earlier. "I stand back and get a good look at it so the tank looks like it belongs there and so it works with the other lines on the bike."

"I look at key areas, how it meets the seat, where it hits the nick. I try to keep the front of the tank aligned with the front of the motor, so there's a sweep from the front of the tank down to the front cylinder and the front pipe. At the back the seat should meet the tank and not be higher than the tank. So the two blend together."

"The front mount is easier to figure out because you can get at it, the rear mount is close to the rear cylinder, so it's harder to get at. I tack the front mount in as one piece so it stays level." (Note the photo sequence.)

Rob figures centerline of the front bracket, then the position of the bracket itself, explaining, "I like to use the actual piece to scribe the line, that way there are fewer surprises later."

After marking out the area Rob drills small holes at each corner and starts in with the cut-off wheel, "I buy these discs that are only 1/32 of an inch thick so it's a real clean, accurate cut."

Once he has a hole, Rob sands the edges with the mini belt sander, working gradually up to the line he scribed earlier. "Once the mount fits, I tack it into place, then cut the center out. Just as a note, when these things get finished they're washed out and then sealed, so we do get all the metal dust out of there."

Next, Rob carefully cuts the center out of the top mount assembly and sands all the edges flush.

The support tube is already mitered where it will meet the bottom of the top tube. With the tank and mount bolted to the bike Rob slides the tube into place and estimates as best he can how long it should be.

Installation of the mounts starts by setting the tank on the bike in what Rob considers the ideal location.

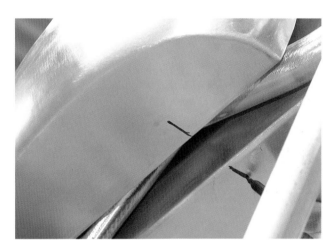

Rob picks an open area along the bottom of the tank for the front mount.

Which is then marked with the dimensions of the mount.

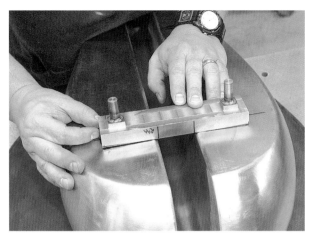

The final position of the mount is checked...

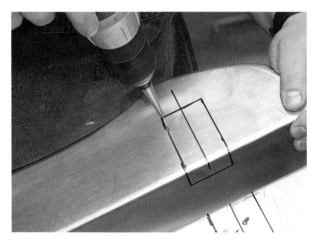

...before Rob cuts small holes in each corner with a step-drill.

The next step is to cut out the rectangle just big enough for the mount to slide in.

"The vertical tube is 1/8 wall DOM, the same stuff we make frames from, so it's a good match in this application. I make sure the tank and mount are positioned where I want them before I tack weld the post in place. The rear mount goes about the same but it's harder because you don't have much room to work."

ROB ROEHL INTERVIEW

Rob Roehl is the long-time metal fabricator for custom-bike builder Donnie Smith. During his time with Donnie, Rob has gone from modifying factory sheet metal, to fabricating components from scratch. From studying How-To Fabricate videos, Rob has graduated to the position of teacher for select groups of students allowed into Donnie's shop for a seminar. What follows are a few of the things Rob has learned during his career as a metal shaper.

Rob, can you give us a little background, explain where you got your training and experience?

I've worked for Donnie Smith for almost 15 years, that's where I got most of my experience. Before that I helped my dad, who raced power boats. At that time you couldn't buy a lot of the stuff we needed so you had to make the parts.

But the biggest turn in my metal shaping was meeting Loren Richards. In a short period of time he moved me ahead years. I owe him a big thank you for teaching me a lot in a short time. Donnie too, he's given me the opportunity to do what I do, he encourages me to take it up another notch. Being a creative guy he understand my need to make each one better than the last one.

How much of your work is building from scratch and how much of it is modifying existing parts?

I do both, 75% is building from scratch, the rest is modifying store-bought stuff. I'd rather fabricate from scratch if possible. Any time I can get a clean sheet of paper it's better than modifying something someone else built or designed.

What type of metal do you prefer to use?

I'm a steel guy, I do some aluminum, not much. For my application, motorcycles, it's the right material. Steel is durable, better for Harley-Davidson type bikes. Sometimes I prototype a part or design in aluminum, but not very often.

Rob cuts the hole just a little small and then files it to fit.

Rob describes this as, "pretty much an 'eye ball' deal."

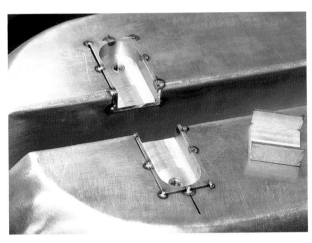

Once the mount is in place Rob cuts it in half...

Which results in a hanging mount welded to the top tube. The pipe is the same material used for frames so it's plenty strong and a good match.

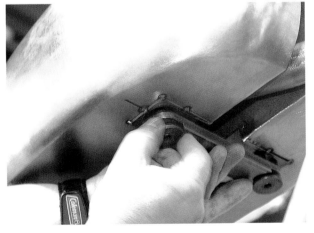

...and mounts the tank on the bike so the position of the frame mount can be determined.

After he's sure of the fit, Rob can remove the tank and final weld the mount to the frame.

The finished mounts, hanging from the top tube..

...ready to mate up with the mounts welded into the bottom of the tank. "You can see so much more of the bottom of the tank on these tall bikes that we've developed this recessed mounting system."

Do you always use a buck?

No, that's rare. Sometimes I just draw it out on cardboard or make a mock up. A lot of times I just make it. I am blessed with the ability to see things ahead of time and get them to look the way I saw them in my head.

I can use the buck we did for this project to make more signature tanks, or as a base shape for other projects. I can use it more than once. Otherwise, a lot of what I do is one-off so there's no point in making a buck. Most times I don't back myself into a corner so bad that I can't get out of it.

What do you have for tools and what do you recommend for other shapers?

I've been a hammer and bag guy for years. I got the power hammer a year ago. Hand hammering takes a toll on you. With the power hammer you can do it quicker with less wear and tear on the body. I've had my wheel for five years and I use it all the time. That was built for my type of work, for what I do. Loren Richards built both my wheel and hammer. Unfortunately he doesn't want to make any more of those hammers.

I think the best way to learn is with a hammer and bag. You get that initial understanding before you start buying power tools. I did it for a long time without a power hammer, 14 years. And I have to say the little hand shrinker/stretchers are great, even for a guy who's only doing this as a hobby.

How do you decide where to put the seams on big projects?

Seam location is dictated by how much shape you can put into a piece without making another piece. It's practical. It revolves around your abilities to shape. If you can't deep-shrink you're going to have to cut and patch and weld.

What's your preference for welding?

You do what you do, what works best for you. I like TIG, it's clean. Wirefeed welders make a hard, dirty weld. I do it all heli-arc, but it's a skill that takes time to learn.

What kind of advice do you have for people starting out, or someone who wants to get better than they are?

The advice I give to people is to be patient. Learn as much about metal shaping as you can and then just be patient. Practice, practice, practice. I look at stuff I did ten years ago and it's almost embarrassing but it's all part of the learning curve.

The hardest part is the patience. Guys like Ron Covell have been doing this work for 30 years. I want everything perfect, it's hard to work to that quality level I set for myself. A lot of people give up because their parts don't look like the parts that Ron or Fay or I do. My Dad said, 'When you figure you've got it figured out, then do something else, because that's all the better you're going to get.'

But if you stick with it you get a reward, like when one of my customers comes in and he sees the piece I've fabricated in the raw and it blows him away. He doesn't even want to paint it.

Bottom view shows the rear mount, the one Rob says "is the hardest to mount by far, just because you don't have much clearance."

The small filler panel seen here will be welded to the frame.

The finished tank, mounted on the frame. Note how it sits just up off the top tube and how the rear of the tank clears the frame tubes.

Classic Metal

From Original Rust to Better than New

The project seen here is the creation of two fenders for a 1922 Rolls Royce. Before the metal work can commence Craig Naff needs to make a buck and that's where this story really starts. Craig introduces us to this project by explaining how the old fender is used to make a buck for the new. "To start I've set the old fender up the way it would sit on the car, then I draw a centerline front to rear and make a cutout that shows the outline of the fender, the profile or side view. I use that to make

Old and new together. In back, the original 1922 Rolls Royce fender. In front, Craig's recreation. By using mirror image techniques one fender can be used to make a buck for both sides.

the outline on the board that will run through the center of the buck. The buck itself is made from 1/2 inch particle board. I cut that center piece out with the jig saw or band saw."

For the next step Craig cuts a base for the buck explaining as he does, "I try to design a buck so I can reverse all the pieces and use it for the other side. It saves all the time of having to make that second buck." With the center piece screwed to the base Craig holds the original cardboard cut out up against the fender and marks a line where the fender lip meets the cardboard. Craig cuts a second template that matches the line of the fender lip exactly.

With the new cardboard pattern he marks and cuts out another piece of particle board that follows the fender lip. This new piece of particle board is screwed to the base, which was cut to be exactly the right width for this project.

Next Craig cuts out a template for the inside of the fender, along the rusty inner edge of the apron. A piece of tape shows where the actual edge of the metal falls, and where the top of the stepped section is. Craig follows the familiar pattern: create a cutout or pattern from cardboard, transfer those measurements to the particle board, then cut the particle board and mount it to the base.

Now the high point of the fender is marked at the very top. This reference point, 90 degrees to the centerline, is the high point of the fender when looked at front-to-rear. Craig carefully creates a template of the fender shape, in cross section, from the high point or center of the centerline to the inner edge, from cardboard. Craig also measures the distance from the centerline piece of the buck to the inner (front-to-rear) panel.

Now Craig installs the first of the side to side stations into the buck, even though this piece is not trimmed yet. The template made earlier from cardboard is used now, to mark the outline of the fender on the station just installed. Once the first station is trimmed Craig attaches it on three sides with more of the sheet rock screws.

To create the next station Craig makes another mark along the centerline on the top of the fender, then uses another piece of cardboard to create the

Craig starts the project by setting the fender up on the bench and then drawing out the front-to-rear centerline.

The next step is to make a cutout that follows the contour of the fender at the centerline.

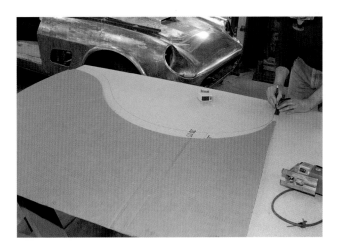

The cardboard cutout is used then to cut the center spine for the buck.

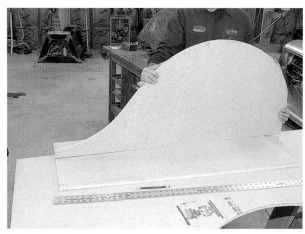

After deciding how wide the base should be, Craig locates the center piece, which will be held in place with sheet rock screws.

A separate piece of cardboard is used to fill in the outline of the fender lip at the rear.

Next, he makes a cutout of the fender lip...

The front-to-rear pieces are attached to the base with sheet rock screws. Craig drills holes in the base along the centerline of each piece.

...which is indexed to the fender itself.

The process continues as Craig makes another template, one that locates the inner edge of the fender.

second template for the second station. Like the first, Craig starts with a rectangle of particle board, then cuts the notch for the support on the inner side, then drills the holes for the sheet rock screws and mounts the new station in place temporarily. Now he traces the shape of the fender onto the station using the template created a few minutes earlier.

"I find that I don't use as many stations as some other fabricators," says Craig. "It's really a matter of personal taste. On this fender it's not changing shape very fast so I don't think you need as many stations. I tend to place them where there's a major shape change, so you would have the station at the highest point. The front station is positioned (note photo of fender profile) right where the curved shape of the fender changes and the radius becomes much tighter."

With that station in place it's time to measure down the centerline of the fender toward the front and create the location for the next station. The distance down the centerline is transferred to the centerline of the buck. Then the rectangular section is created. As before, Craig creates a cardboard profile of the fender at that station location, and transfers that shape to the station with a pencil, then cuts it with a jig saw. Any necessary trimming is done with a sanding block.

After the second station is cut and installed the process becomes repetitive. It turns out you have to be a bit of a carpenter to be a good metal fabricator. Working toward the rear of the fender the last station is placed where the fender changes shape, where it goes from a compound curve to a simple curve just before it meets the running board.

Craig explains that making the stations for the outside of the fender is done in much the same way as the inside, "I will use pretty much the same location (front to rear) for these but shift each one ahead or behind 3/4 inch to leave room for the screw heads."

The process starts at the highest part of the fender, Craig uses the same basic techniques seen earlier to build the stations. Each one starts as a rectangle of particle board, cut to slide between the center rib of the buck and the outside piece (the

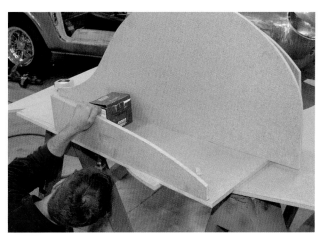

The baseboard is exactly the right width so the inner part of the buck goes up against the edge.

The first station will be positioned at the fender's highest point.

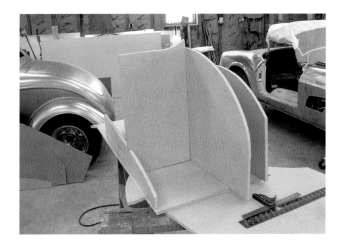

Here you can see the station - which will have to be removed again after Craig cuts a template of the fender's side-to-side contour.

Working at the highest point on the fender Craig makes a template that matches the shape exactly.

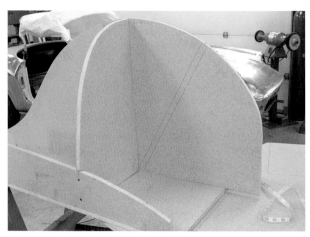

...before being reunited with the rest of the buck.

Then transfers that shape to the station..

Each station requires that Craig create a template of the shape.

...which is removed from the buck and cut along the contour line...

Then a station is installed in the buck at the same location.

And then the template made earlier is used to transfer the contour of the fender to the station.

Each station is first installed, then marked and cut along the contour line before being reinstalled.

After creating stations for the inside of the fender, Craig goes through the same process for the outside.

fender lip piece). After trimming and notching each rectangle it is screwed temporarily in place, then the contour or profile of the fender is transferred to the new station, it is removed, then cut along the line drawn from the template and reinstalled.

The final part of making the buck is to cut a big hole in the outside panel, "this is for access," explains Craig, "so I can see up inside the buck and tell whether or not the panel is sitting on the stations."

In this way and over the better part of a day, Craig creates a complete buck for the creation of the fender. "I don't hammer on these bucks," he adds, "That's a whole different process. I only use these for checking the shape." After trimming with a sanding block the buck is finished.

WHERE TO PUT THE SEAMS

When it comes to deciding where to put the seams Craig explains, "I try to split the areas with the most shape." Once he knows where the seams will be, Craig can measure along the centerline piece, then side to side, and transfer those dimensions to the raw sheet steel.

Craig only makes a paper pattern for certain parts of the fender, "because the center part of the fender is a pretty regular shape I skip that pattern step. But I will make a pattern for the very front of the fender and some of the other areas too."

"The metal I use here is plain old steel. This is 18 gauge cold-rolled steel, it's all I've ever used. Ron Covell says to try the A-K but then I might get spoiled. And to get any of that material I'd probably have to buy a whole pallet. I use mostly power tools so it's not as critical to me as it might be for some other people."

After cutting the front corners off Craig washes the piece to eliminate the skin of oil and dust on the steel, and marks the line of demarcation separating the area of maximum shrinking from the rest of the panel.

Stations for the outside of the fender are staggered slightly from those on the inside.

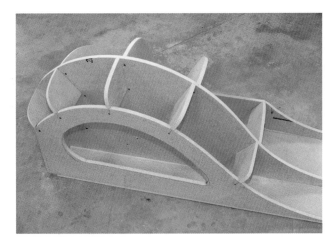

Note the cutout in the outside of the buck, which makes it easier to see up inside and ensure the metal is touching all the stations.

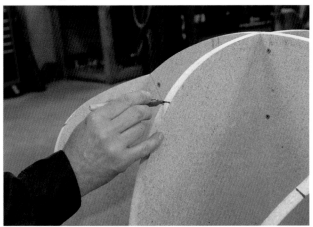

After the buck is finished Craig can begin laying out the panels and the location of each seam.

SHRINKING

Then he installs the shrinking dies in the Pullmax and starts in shrinking with thumbnail dies. Next Craig switches to the Eckold, explaining as he does, "The advantage of using the two machines is I can put gathering-type shrinking dies in the Eckold and smooth out the wrinkles left by the Pullmax while I'm still shrinking." Craig continues to work the edges, right up to and past the "line" drawn on the metal, with the Eckold.

Craig switches to the power hammer and stretching dies. "Now I have to bring the center up to get everything else to go down, if I continue to shrink it will just wrinkle up the edges."

TEST FIT

After that round of shrinking and stretching it's time for a test fit. "The only place it's touching the buck is in a narrow strip along the middle," explains Craig. "So if I raise the top more the sides will come down more until they touch the buck."

Now Craig goes back to the power hammer with the stretching dies. Then a test fit. The rate of change is slow now, the panel still doesn't wrap down enough at the edges. Craig marks an area in the center toward the back of the panel, that area needs to come up more, and then heads back for the power hammer. Another test fit, working along the transition area where it goes from stretching to shrinking.

Craig moves to the Eckold shrinker working mostly the edges followed by another test fit. What we see is lots of change from a small amount of shrinking. Another test fit shows the sides have come down considerably and the fit is much better.

Now Craig goes back to the Pettingell power hammer, explaining "We need dies that aren't so flat, so we can get out toward the curved area of the fender more."

At this point the project turns into a long series of test fits and power hammer sessions.

The test fit shows it to be over-shrunk a little, so Craig stretches it some along the edge again where it starts to turn down. Another test fit shows it to have lifted a little off the buck at the sides, but overall it's better. This test shows it to be rocking on the buck at the back in the center, so Craig stretches, or lifts it, in that area.

Rather than make a full paper pattern, Craig simply measures the width and length of the panel and cuts out a sheet of steel.

Craig makes 2 passes around the metal, going all the way to the edge of the shrinking area, then one more going about half that far in.

Paper patterns are used only for difficult areas like the very nose of the fender.

This is what the front of the fender looks like after the first round of shrinking with a thumbnail die in the Pullmax machine.

Craig starts the shaping process by shrinking all the way around the blank. Note the line that marks the edge of the shrinking area.

Frequent test fits are all part of the process and prevent Craig from going too far with one part of the fender.

Craig continues to shrink, but with a pair of gathering type dies in the Eckold. This way he can shrink and eliminate wrinkles at the same time.

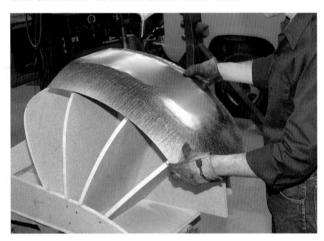

Another test fit. The piece has come a long way in a short period of time.

The nose has a lot of shape and requires further shrinking.

We are getting close, after another test fit Craig declares, "it's fitting good at the front station but not too well farther back, so I'm going to raise that area to help the rest of it fit the buck. Part of the trouble is the way this fender rolls so much at the very front." The marks Craig makes on the fender are notes, telling him where to stretch and where to shrink.

He does just a little shrinking at either front corner, then more stretching, concentrating on a band running across the front of the fender. A test fit shows progress. The contour is coming along, though it's still off the stations some at the inside edge. Which means more stretching and more checking,

There's a tough-to-shape area between the first and second station on the inside where the fender goes from a lot of shape to an almost flat section as it makes the transition to the apron. Craig does a lot of fine tuning at this point, a little shrinking at the two front corners for example to get the tip to roll down more. Then more stretching all through the center of the piece.

After a break Craig starts the next session by installing a new lower die, one with a three inch radius, in the power hammer, explaining as he does, "I need to take the corner out of the curve on the outside, give it a more gradual curved shape." After working the area with the Pettingell it's time for another test fit.

Sometimes in areas where the edge doesn't come down far enough to meet the buck, Craig will stretch it, even though logic would suggest that the better way to do it is to shrink. "Sometimes I over-shrink an area and it will raise the area behind it, so then I have to go back and stretch it a little bit so the shrinking is relaxed and the raised area can come down." After doing exactly what is described above the outside of the fender matches the buck almost perfectly.

Craig changes to a six inch radius lower die because, "With the smaller die you really concentrate the power and move a lot of metal quickly." After a test fit Craig marks the areas that need to come up or be raised, then changes to a five inch radius followed by more power hammer work on the Pettingell. Then a little shrinking at the very nose and the corners of the fender to roll the tip down more.

This fender section is almost finished, Craig uses his hand to help identify high and low areas he can't pick up by eye. Again, he marks those areas with a red marker and then goes back to the power hammer for a little more stretching.

When the piece is done Craig takes it over to the planishing hammer. After applying a little spray lube the piece is run through between a pair of fairly flat dies to eliminate the hills and valleys in the metal's surface.

The planishing hammer does move metal, however, "just not as much or as fast as the power hammer." So Craig has to anticipate the metal's movement during the finishing stages. As an example he explains, "At our last fitting you could see the area in the middle needed to be raised more. But I left it low because I knew it would come up after we used the planishing hammer. Now the fit is pretty good, but the edges seem a little over-shrunk. That's OK though because those will relax a little after being run through the planishing hammer."

A good metal fabricator is forced to think ahead. It's not enough to get the shape perfect, you also have to consider the effects of the finishing operations on the contours you've created. Craig warns that you need to be careful when you're almost finished with a panel, "So you don't try to move the metal too far too fast, or you might be forced to start over. At the beginning of the project it's easier to correct for mistakes, near the end it's not."

Now a fairly crowned set of dies is installed and used to relax the outside edge and corner. The work on the outer edge with the more crowned dies caused the outside edge to relax and lay right down tight against the buck.

Now to the wheel, "to get some ripples out of the inside and also stretch that area just a little so it won't rock on the buck, and a little on the other side to smooth out the area with the sharp curve at the outside edge." All with moderate pressure on the wheel.

With a curved section like the outside edge, you have to use a planishing die with a lot of

Though the fender looks good so far, it's only touching the buck along a narrow center strip...

...the answer is to raise the center with stretching dies in the Pettingell power hammer.

By raising the center area the edges will come down closer to the buck.

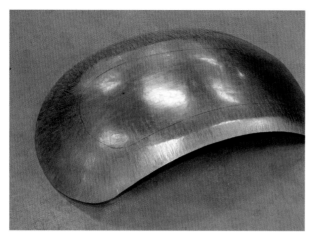

Though it looks pretty good the front of the fender still doesn't sit tight on all the stations.

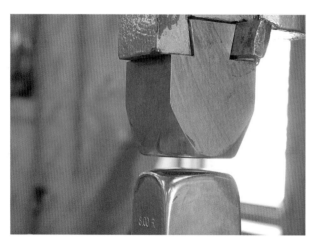

This lower die with an 8 inch radius is what Craig used for much of the stretching done through the center of the fender.

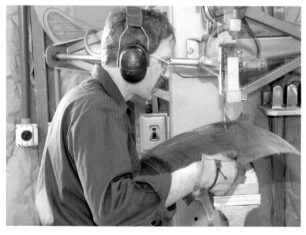

Here Craig works the transition area where the metal goes from stretched to shrunk.

crown. It is difficult to get a smooth finish with a high-crown die.

Craig declares the piece almost done, "the outer edge isn't quite finished but I've got to go in and add another piece to it later so there's no point in making it perfect right now." At this point the front edge has been left a little too long so there is enough metal to wrap a wire (a process that comes later).

THE NEXT PIECE OF THE PUZZLE

With the original paper pattern Craig checks the location of the side apron. With paper on the buck and pins in the places where the seam is located, Craig marks the edge, then transfers the measurements to the metal.

Now the newly cut piece of metal is held up against the buck and a line is marked that repre-

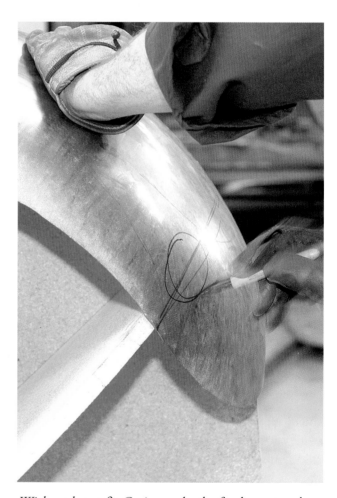

With each test fit Craig marks the fender as to what it needs and where. In this case what's needed is more stretching across the front...

sents the limit of the shrinking. The operation starts with the Pullmax, much as before, with the same dies. Craig follows the same procedure: first he makes two passes across the panel with the shrinker, going full depth each time, followed by another two that only go half way to the edge-of-shrinking line marked earlier.

The Eckold is next as Craig continues shrinking with the gathering-type dies. Note the dramatic and speedy way in which the big wrinkles are eliminated. This piece shapes fairly easily. Now he does a little power hammer work, using a die with an eight inch radius crown, which just happens to match the mild crown on the inside of the fender where it fades to the apron.

The piece is getting close, so Craig clamps it to the buck and then does a careful analysis of the progress. After making a few "notes" with red marker he goes back to the power hammer with the same eight inch die working the areas just marked.

ANOTHER TEST FIT

The part is not touching at the top, especially toward the front. Craig does a little shrinking along the edge and some stretching with the power hammer on areas that are touching the buck and holding the rest of the piece from fitting up tight. This process of getting the piece to lie up against all the surfaces of the buck involves many test fits and sessions with (mostly) the power hammer. At the end of the day the inner piece fits pretty well but it still isn't perfect.

One of the paper patterns Craig does use is a tracing from the front edge of the inner fender. Using this pattern Craig trims the panel at the front, commenting as he does, "I left about an extra inch so I'd have plenty of metal to wrap the edge wire."

A test fit shows the upper edge, especially toward the rear, rolls too quick. It's only hitting at the edge of the buck and not in the middle of the curve so Craig takes the piece over to the power hammer and stretches the metal in a band two inches from the edge. This relaxes the whole area, softens the curve and helps that area better match the contour of the buck. The same basic technique is used across much of the panel in order to soften

...done on the Pettingell with an 8 inch-radius lower die.

Another test fit shows the fender section as nearly finished, only a few problem areas remain.

Like the "corner" in the contour on the outside edge, which is smoothed out with a 3 inch-radius die.

At the end of the project the progress seems to slow down. The final fine-tuning includes raising the center of the fender with a 5 inch-radius die.

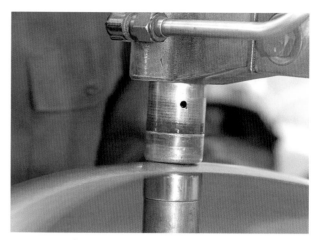

...equipped with a set of pretty flat dies.

To get the edges at the front to roll down more Craig does some additional shrinking.

The English wheel is used for two reasons: To smooth out imperfections left after the planishing...

The finishing starts with a few passes through the planishing hammer...

...and to stretch areas just in from the edge that need to be raised slightly.

the crown and help achieve a shape that matches the buck exactly.

Finally the inner panel fits all the stations except the one in the middle, causing Craig to comment, "it's fitting everywhere else so I'm going to let it go. The position of that one station might be off a little and we've got a nice smooth curve running across here and that's what you want. Sometimes you've got to trust your eye." Near the end Craig sharpens the radius at the very back of the panel by working it over a couple of dollies.

Time now to finish the panel. Once again Craig will anticipate the effects of finishing on the shape. It's still a little too tight overall and doesn't quite come up against the stations all across their surface, so if the finishing relaxes the panel just a little bit, that's fine.

The first step in finishing is done on the power hammer with a fairly flat die, one with an 18 inch radius. Next comes the planishing hammer and a few tweaks by hand until eventually the inner panel lays up against the buck the way it should.

PIECE NUMBER THREE

Time now to make the third panel in this multi-panel project. Rather than make a paper template, Craig simply measures the distances on the buck and transfers those dimensions to the sheet steel.

He starts the shaping by hand, by simply bending the steel. Then Craig marks off various areas depending on which shaping techniques are required. Like the outside areas that need shrinking and the inside area, or crown, that requires stretching.

Craig begins the shaping on the Pullmax where the shrinking die makes quick work of the marked areas on either side. "I want to get this area to fit fairly well before I go to the other side, I don't want to get too far ahead of myself."

After doing the raw shrinking Craig moves to the Eckold to continue shrinking while smoothing out the lumpy surface left by the thumbnail die on the Pullmax. Craig stops before going too far, or the piece will be picked up right off the buck.

The fit of the front part of the fender on the buck is close enough that Craig decides to move on to the next piece.

When checked against the paper template the front of the fender proves to be a little long, but that's OK as we need extra metal for edge wiring.

For the creation of the inner fender Craig does form a full paper template.

After cutting the mild steel sheet to the correct size Craig marks the limit of the area that he will shrink.

Here you can see in a series of steps...

Shrinking starts with the thumbnail dies in the Pullmax

...how the Eckold is used again...

You can see how Craig made two passes, running the metal all the way to the marked edge of shrinking, then did another where he only went half way.

...to smooth out the ripples while adding to the crown.

After shrinking both the outside and inside Craig moves to the power hammer, with a five-inch-radius die, and works along the outside edge. This relaxes the edge on the outside rear and allows the panel to lie closer to the buck. The same procedure is used on the inside of the fender at the rear, to the same effect - the panel was a little over-shrunk prior to the power hammer work.

The next major step in the process is to stretch the metal all through the middle of the panel using the power hammer and the same die with a five inch radius.

After a test fit Craig continues with the Pettingell, stretching the center and smoothing out the transition from the softly crowned top to the more sharply curved sides.

More test fits and more stretching follow for a good 40 Minutes....

In a relatively short time the panel is essentially finished. Craig moves to the wheel to roll a nice transition area between the outer edge and the flat reverse-curve area at the back of the fender. "It works better than the hammer, which tends to leave the surface a series of flat sections."

Craig changes to a 10 inch radius die and uses it to raise the area just ahead of the reverse curve. This area between the two edges is now slightly concave and should be raised slightly. This is a difficult area to shape, as the metal in the center must go from crowned to a reverse curve.

A flatter wheel is installed and Craig works the rearward edge on the inside where the shrinking ends and the panel flattens out. This is very similar to what was done in the same area on the other side.

This panel is nearly finished. Craig stretches and shrinks small areas very carefully with many test fits and painstakingly gets the panel to sit on the buck and meet all the stations. At the end it's very much like a careful massage. Craig slides the edge of the metal between the shrinker jaws just long enough for a few gentle blows, then pulls it out for another test fit.

Where other fabricators seem to force the metal into submission, Craig encourages the metal to move.

Using a die with mild radius Craig begins stretching the inner fender or apron.

Next comes a test fit which shows the piece to be very nearly finished.

Using a paper template Craig marks the outline at the front of the inner fender, leaving a little extra metal for the edge-wiring that will come later.

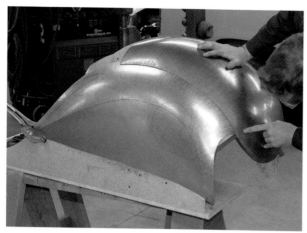

A test fit done with the front section shows the inner fender/apron to be touching at the top and front, but not in the middle.

At this point the inner fender fits well, exhibits a nice shape, and blends well where it meets the front fender section.

The answer is to stretch the apron where it was shrunk earlier to raise and relax the area.

Time for piece number 3. .After cutting out the blank, shaping starts very much by hand.

Before declaring the piece finished Craig does a little detail work with hammer and dolly at the very back corner.

After the rough shape is established Craig does an analysis of the part and marks areas that need shrinking or stretching.

The hammer and dolly are used to eliminate some small dents at the back of the panel. Then Craig finishes shaping the end of the panel on the Eckold with a new set of dies, duralon upper and T-dolly lower, to roll the edge (see pics) then install stretching dies and stretch the same outer edge slightly. Now it is finally time for planishing and a little tweaking. Finishing this piece was made more difficult because of the transition area where the crowned center strip meets the flat reverse curve, with the crowned and shrunk areas on either side. Each little change in any one spot has profound consequences over a big area.

Craig attaches both front and rear panels to the buck to ensure they fit and fit together. He marks a line where they overlap and trims the upper piece nice and clean, then puts it back on the buck, "You have to be sure they meet nice and neat, I don't want to be stretching or shrinking that area afterward. When I'm trimming I bend the scrap piece up and out of the way as I go to minimize distortion of the main piece."

The two panels are joined by a series of tack welds, with hammer and dolly work after every couple of tacks. Craig does use filler rod for these tack welds. (.040, 70 S6 rod, with the welder set to DC straight polarity, 55 to 60 amps approximately).

Final welding is done in one inch strips, spaced out across the seam. After the four short bursts of welding, Craig hammer and dollys each one with a dolly that matches the contour of the fender. Then another series of one inch welds and another round of hammer and dolly work. In this way Craig works his way across the fender, creating a seam that is both strong and true to the overall shape of the fender.

Time now to join the side panel/apron to the rest of the fender. Before attaching the apron to the fender however, Craig cleans up the edge with a DA sander. After checking to ensure the transition area where the apron meets the fender edge is smooth, Craig decides to simply hold the apron in place and then scribe a line on the "fender." The cutting is done with a tin snips.

In a familiar pattern, Craig starts with shrinking in the Pullmax...

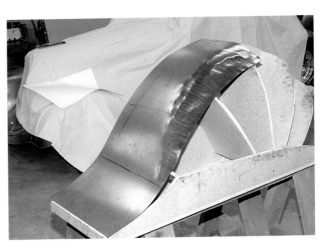

...and then does a test fit...

...followed by smoothing and more shrinking in the Eckold machine.

The test fit showed the need for more shrinking at the edge.

Time now to stretch and raise up the band of metal through the center.

Which must be smoothed out with the Eckold before...

Transition areas are difficult, like this area where the crowned areas meet the flat section on the back of the fender.

...the next test fit.

Off the buck the piece appears to be nearly finished.

After tack welding the finish welding begins. Again, Craig does a series of one inch welds, well spaced, with hammer and dolly work after every group of three or four. In this way he welds the entire seam from back to front with very little distortion. What's left is the installation of the outside panel and the edge wiring of the fender.

THE LAST PANEL

The edge wire used here is 3/16 inch mild steel rod. Craig combines edge wiring with the creation of the last, outside panel needed to complete the fender. As he explains, "It's much easier to put the edge-wire in place before the panel is shaped, rather than the other way around."

"The rule of thumb for edge wiring is: You need 2-1/2 times the diameter of the wire. In this case that's 15/32 of an inch from the edge."

Craig makes two marks, one at 15/32 and one at 3/16 of an inch from the edge, then uses those marks as guides as the strip of metal is placed in the break. The double bend forms a U channel, into which Craig slips the wire, which is initially trapped as Craig rolls the edge over with a body hammer.

To finish closing the metal around the wire he installs a special set of dies in the Pullmax and runs the edge of the fender through three times. The result is a very neat, clean edge wrapped tight around the wire.

After running the panel through the dies Craig starts the shaping by stretching the upper section first. The stretching causes the piece to form a definite curve. After a test fit Craig does another round of stretching before using the shrinking dies to encourage the metal to curve the other way at the back of the fender.

Some parts of the new panel pick up a little crown in cross section, "because the dies can only reach back as far as the wire." Craig eliminates the crown by running the piece through the planishing hammer.

Getting the panel to follow the outline of the fender is a matter of patiently stretching and shrinking with plenty of test fitting between. The long narrow shape of the panel means that it often picks up a twist during all this shrinking and

To create a nice rolled edge along the back of the fender Craig uses the English wheel.

To lift the area just ahead of the flat section Craig stretches the metal with the power hammer

To roll the inside edge Craig uses the wheel again, but with a different anvil wheel than was used on the other side.

At the end of the fender a special T-dolly lower, and soft upper, die are used to create a better rolled edge.

A test fit shows a good match between the three main panels of the fender.

Here you can see how nice the edge fits the buck.

With the panels trimmed and clamped carefully in place Craig can start to tack weld the three panels together.

The planishing hammer is used to finish the surface and do a little more stretching.

The tack welds are spaced carefully and cause no warpage of the panels or seam.

stretching. Craig eliminates the twist by simply hammering the piece flat on the bench.

The fact that we are trying to make the metal follow the edge of the buck points out the importance of making an accurate buck in the first place.

After the basic shape of the side panel is correct Craig needs to determine the exact shape of the front of the fender, because that edge must still be "wired" and the two panels have to come together smoothly. Craig uses a paper template to mark the new fender with the outline of the old.

Craig bends the front of the long panel until it starts to sweep over toward the center of the car, then clamps the panel in place, marks and trims away any excess metal. Dies in the Pullmax are used to create the mild crown on the new panel.

Craig scribes a line on the main fender now, then moves it to the bench and trims to the line with a tin snips. Next the outer strip is checked for fit and tack welded in place. The tacking starts at the front with a series of small fusion welds. For each weld Craig first moves the loose part of the fender around so the gap is tight, positions the welding tip close to the seam and then hits the gas. If the weld holds he readjusts the remaining strip of metal, does another fusion weld, and starts all over again.

Once the entire strip is attached with the small welds and the fitment is deemed good, Craig starts to do the final welding in short segments spread across the seam. The short weld segments produce very minimal warpage, the seams don't open up and they don't tighten up. One piece of metal isn't trying to jump up over another as a result of too much heat. The entire seam is welded up in this slow, patient fashion with hammer and dolly work after each series of welds is finished.

WIRED

At this point the front of the fender is pretty raw and needs a bit of massaging to create a nice accurate edge that encloses the wire. Finishing the fender edge starts as Craig wraps the wire behind the center of the fender and clamps it in place. Next, he scribes a line that represents the eventual end of the fende. Now Craig tack welds the wire to the two panels. despite the fact that there is consid-

Final welding of the seam is done in one inch increments. After doing a series of these welds, Craig hammer and dollys the entire seam...

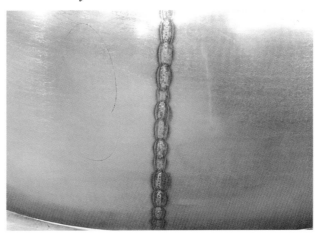

...then goes back and does another series of one inch welds.

Once the seam running across the fender is final-welded, Craig scribes and trims the area where the inner fender meets the main fender.

This seam too is first tack welded, then final-welded in one inch strips.

For the outer lip Craig cuts a narrow strip of steel and a piece of edge wire just a little bit longer.

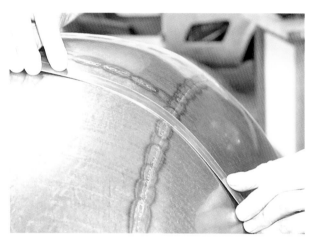

The ruler shows just how nice the seam is after final welding and a little hammer and dolly work.

Craig makes two marks before placing the sheet of steel in the break...

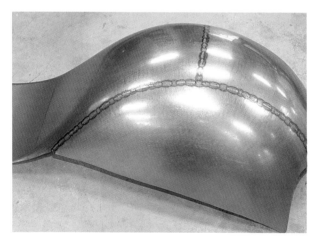

The fender appears finished, but only if you're looking at the inside.

...and carefully bending a neat U-shaped channel just big enough for the edge wire.

erable overlap between the two panels (check the photos here to relieve confusion).

Craig heat shrinks the outside flap of metal, causing it to suck up tight against the main part of the fender. To cut out the overlapping metal, Craig uses a die cutter to create a cut, then inserts the blade from a powered keyhole saw. Now the new seam can be welded in the fashion illustrated earlier.

The tape line he runs across the front is just under 1/2 inch, or very close to 15/32 inch. Craig then trims to tape edge. Where there's not quite enough metal to have a full 15/32nd tab Craig welds a small extension on the edge of the metal. Now with just enough extra metal extending past the "end" of the fender Craig can enclose the wire.

With specially modified vise grips Craig bends a tab back a little past 90 degrees. This is done in a series of smaller steps working across the front and inside edge of the fender. With the fender flipped onto its side Craig now works the tab with hammer and dolly, gradually working it into more of a U shape.

After the U-channel is fully formed Craig cuts a piece of wire a little too long for the intended application. "Any unevenness you see along that edge can be eliminated when we put the wire in and fold the metal over the wire," explains Craig. "If you hold your hands well apart and bend the wire gently you get much nicer bends than if you put your hands close together and just muscle the wire." After being shaped the wire is clamped in place, marked where it meets the other wire (which was trimmed earlier) and then the two wires are welded together. This must be done without any build up or it will affect how neatly the sheet metal can be rolled over the wire.

Craig starts with the vise grip, folding the metal over enough to hold the wire in place, then comes the hammer and dolly. Once he has one area full wrapped around the wire he just continues down the wire.

If the piece is too big to go into the Pullmax the final crimp must be done with a specially modified vise grip working from one end of the wire to the other. Now it's time to cut off the excess wire and declare the fender finished.

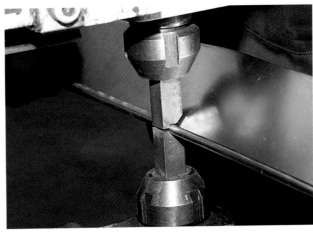

Final "closing" of the sheet metal around the edge wire is done with this special tooling in the Pullmax...

...which leaves the edge of the fender with a very nice "factory" finish.

The shaping starts after the installation of the wire - in this case by stretching the upper edge which quickly puts a curve in the narrow panel.

The first test fit shows the need for more shaping, especially toward the rear of the fender.

Craig installs shrinking dies in the Eckold and shrinks the end of the fender-edge...

...which causes it to turn up and follow the rest of the fender.

Because the wire will run all the way across the fender, Craig plans the "wiring" of both the inner fender...

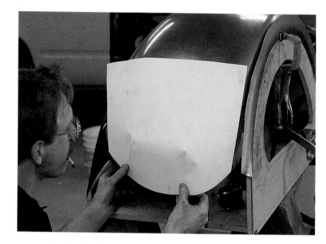

...and the fender tip, with templates made from the original fender.

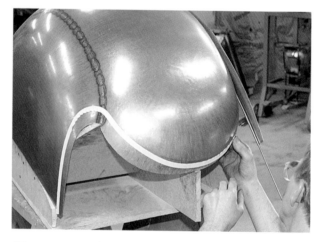

Here a piece of tape is used to mark the edge of the fender, leaving enough extra metal to wrap around the wire.

CRAIG NAFF INTERVIEW

Since making the move from conventional body work to metal fabrication twenty some years ago, Craig Naff has done a wide variety of work. From CadZZilla built in the Boyd Coddington shop for Billy Gibbons to the 32 Chevrolet cover car built by Larry Erickson (who designed CadZZilla by the way) Craig Naff has built everything from high dollar hot rods to restoration parts for old classics.

Like most metal working shops, Craig Naff's is crowded with cars and projects in various states of completion. Unlike a lot of shops, Craig's is very neat and contains both classics and hot rods. Near the door sits a Ferrari in bare metal, ready to go back to the nearby specialty shop for assembly, while a small group of hot rods occupy the remaining floor space.

Among the hot rods is a roadster with the lines of a 33 Ford. The car is Craig's creation, from the chassis to the body and running boards. The only part of the body that Craig didn't fabricate from scratch is a small section of quarter panel on either rear corner. As if it weren't enough to build a complete body and chassis, Craig also designed and built the dash, including the instrument cluster and convex glass dome. Even the taillight housings and lenses are Craig's design and fabrication.

When it comes to shaping sheet metal and fabricating parts, it doesn't appear there are very many things that Craig Naff can't do.

Craig, can we start with some background on you and how you came to be a metal shaper?

I started with auto body classes in high school. After that I worked at a Ford dealership body shop. Then I worked for White Post Restoration near Winchester, Virginia from 1979 to 1983. When I worked there the body people were responsible for all the body work on a particular car. That included the metal fabrication. But the shop owner liked my metal work and pretty soon he had me doing all the metal work. I just self taught myself the trade as I did more and more metal work.

By 1984 I was married to Kathy and working out of my own shop in Asheboro, North Carolina. I built a car there that won the Grand National

Getting the fender edge into precisely the right shape requires a certain amount of good old-fashioned hand work.

After scribing a line on the the fender edge where it meets the rest of the fender, the excess metal is trimmed away.

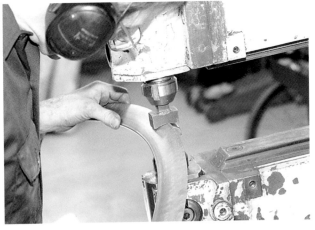

To create a soft crown in the narrow strip of metal, Craig uses a set of dies with exactly that radius, in the Pullmax.

119

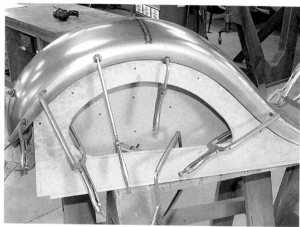

Once it's trimmed and shaped, the fender edge can be clamped in place. There is still an overlap where the two surfaces overlap...

As before, the finish welding is done in one-inch increments. Note how nice and tight the gap is - after the welding.

...so Craig scribes a line and carefully trims away the excess metal.

The nearly finished fender, missing only the edge wiring at the front tip and a bit of finishing.

Once a nice clean butt-joint is established, it's time to tack weld the two pieces together.

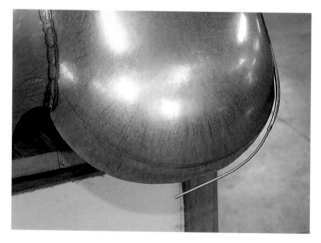

Getting the wire to run smoothly from the fender edge across the tip requires patience and a lot of hand work.

award at the Hot Rod Nationals in 1984. Boyd Coddington saw that car and pretty soon he started calling. Six weeks later we decided to go to California and work for Boyd. That was in 1986. We stayed there until 1989 when Kathy and I moved back to Virginia.

Once I moved here I did some Ferrari work. The first one required 75 percent new panels. Today I do both hot rods and restoration work, about 75 percent hot rods and custom motorcycles with the remainder being restoration work. I even do a little architectural metal work.

Which do you prefer, hot rod or restoration work and why?

I prefer the hot rods because of the creative element. There is always some design interpretation.

Is it necessary to have a good eye in order to be a good metal fabricator?

I think it is. Even when you're working from an accurate part, you still may need to interpret the shape because the original part is damaged or in poor condition.

Advanced Sheet metal means bigger more complex shapes. Can you talk about the seams. How does a person decide where to put the seams and how does he or she decide how many pieces to make an individual part out of?

As far as size, it's determined by the size you are comfortable handling, or the capacity of the equipment. Seams can be determined by the shape of the part itself. Often I try to divide a shape so you don't have to do all the shaping on one panel, to make the project more manageable and the panels easier to shape.

The Rolls Royce fender was made through a combination of shrinking and stretching. Do you try to use each technique in equal amounts or does it depend on the project?

Well, it's harder to shrink so I tend to stretch more. But you can't do so much stretching that you over-thin the metal.

Let's talk about welding. Bigger pieces mean more seams, how important is welding to sheet metal fabrication and is a TIG welder essential?

Welding is extremely important. You want to create minimal distortion. A TIG welder is essential

At this point Craig wraps the wire behind the fender tip...

...clamps it in place and scribes a line that represents what will be the edge of the finished fender.

To get the strip from the narrow fender edge to pull up tight against the rest of the fender, Craig heat-shrinks just that area.

Metal from the fender edge that overlaps the main fender is trimmed away with the cut-off saw.

Then a powered keyhole saw is used to cut a nice neat seam between the two pieces.

After welding up the seam Craig runs tape across the fender to mark both the cut-off point and the eventual edge of the finished fender.

Forming a U-channel across the front of the fender is done by hand. The process starts as Craig bends the metal back with a modified Vise Grips.

To finish forming the U-channel Craig uses a hammer and dolly with just the right shape.

More vise grips are used to hold everything in place and begin closing the metal over the wire.

to me, I don't like MIG welds. I like gas better than MIG. MIG leaves lots of weld build-up. The welds are brittle and hard to work with.. You have more precise control with the TIG welder.

Concerning aluminum and steel, do you prefer one over the other or does the project determine the metal?

For fenders I prefer steel for the durability. They don't get dinged-up by gravel. Otherwise I don't have much preference. With aluminum you have to compensate for the lack of strength in engineering the part.

Is there one skill or ability that's more important than all the others when it comes to sheet metal fabrication?

They all have to work together so I can't say one is more important than another.

Tools, what is it about power tools that you like?

Partly speed, partly the fact that they're less physically demanding and not as hard on your body.

What does a young person need to get started on a career as a metal shaper?

Patience.

Tight corners like this require the use of a hammer to roll the edge over the wire...

...though the final closing around the wire must be done by hand using another home-made tool.

Any further finishing will be left to the body and paint shop - at this point Craig declares the fender finished.

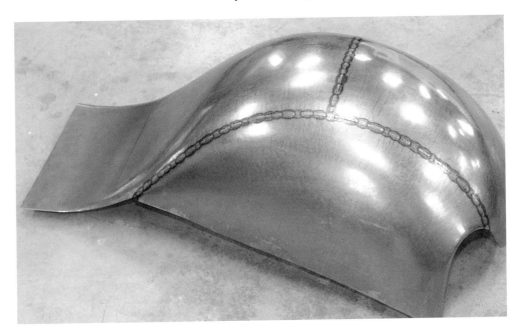

Chapter Six - Mike Pavletic

Art from Italy

Hand Built Panel for a Hand Built Car

Installing a patch panel in an old roadster might seem like the simplest of jobs. Unless the car in question is a rare 1948 AlfaRomeo with an aluminum body by Pininfarina, one of only two built and the only one surviving.

"Originally these cars were hammered out from sheet aluminum by hand," explains Mike, "and planished to eliminate the rough surface. We're going to make the rear body panel out of 1100 aluminum. Essentially that is pure aluminum. The gauge we're using is the same gauge as the rest of the body - .050 inch. That's what

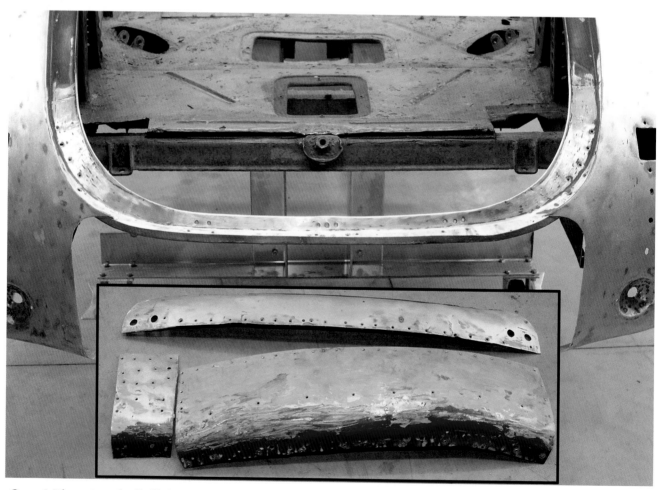

Once Mike stripped off all the old filler, he found an old poorly done repair made up of three separate pieces. Mike also had to cut out the support structure from inside the trunk so he cold fabricate, and finish, the new panel. Once the panels work is done he will fabricate a new support structure.

I'm using because that's probably what the car is made with, those panels are really soft. I don't use a buck for a project like this. If you have a piece to go by you don't need a buck. The existing piece becomes the buck. Sometimes you end up with more time and money in the buck than the part."

CUT THE SHEET

Mike starts by measuring the old piece and then figures out how much to compensate for any shrinking that needs to be done. The lines he draws on the new piece show where the shrinking die will stop (at the first line) and where the area of maximum crown is (between the two lines). "You get an edge or shelf at the edge of the die," says Mike, "and that will be the area of maximum crown."

After two sessions of shrinking, with checking between, Mike declares it's time to do just one more bit of shrinking so the limit of the area affected by the die is right on the line closest to the edge. Then it's time to stretch the area where the panel starts to turn under to get it to roll a bit more.

With the shrinking and the first round of stretching, the piece is coming around. Mike pulls the edge up more, so it rolls more, and that flattens the new piece slightly. "This metal is still pretty soft, even after I've shaped it" explains Mike. "If I had done this on a little hand shrinker, cold-shrinking, the piece would end up a lot more brittle than when you use shrinking dies in a hammer."

Mike explains that sometimes you need to trust your eye. "The original panel is so rough that I'm going to follow my eye more than I am the original piece." The first stretching dies that Mike uses are pretty sharp. After getting enough roll in the area of maximum radius, Mike changes to stretching dies with a low crown. With these dies Mike works the entire panel to put a soft crown in the whole thing.

Mike uses lots of test fits, (note the picture of the panel from the inside). At this point the

No paper pattern is used here, Mike simply measures and cuts the sheet of aluminum. He does mark the edge of shrinking on the new panel.

The aluminum is the same thickness as that on the car. Note the guide marks on the metal.

Mike encourages the metal to take on the proper shape with a little armstrong work.

This is what our piece looks like after two rounds of shrinking...

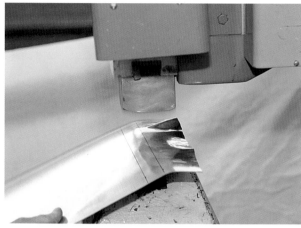

More shrinking is required, here you can see how the dies raise a "pucker" of metal...

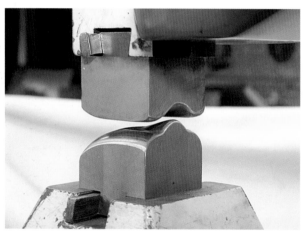

...in these familiar thumbnail dies. Before the test fit Mike will pass the panel through the dies one more time.

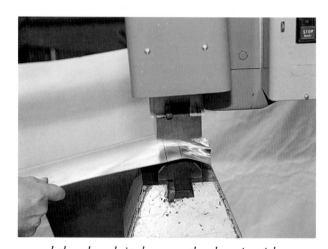

...and then knock it down as the sheet is withdrawn.

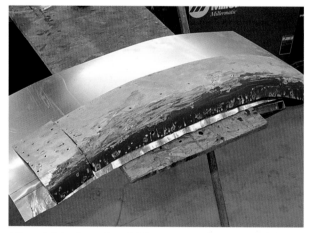

Here Mike lays the old lower-panels on top of the new panel to check the fit and the way the panel rolls at the edge.

Another look at the panel, note how the whole piece has picked up a crown.

panel needs a little more shrinking so Mike changes dies again and takes the puckers out of the edge. Then he checks the fit again and trims off the excess. The piece is getting close but still needs to wrap a little tighter to the upper framework, "but that's just a matter of form, not shape," explains Mike. (Note Fay Butler's comments on form and shape.)

FINISH IT ON THE PLANISHING HAMMER

"Now we can finish it off with the planishing hammer," says Mike. With aluminum you can do a lot of shaping with the planishing hammer because the metal is so soft. With the planishing hammer we're getting a little more crown across the panel, but mostly we're eliminating all

The first test fit simply confirms that Mike has the panel moving in the right direction.

This is the second set of stretching dies used early in the project, the "low-crown die" used to begin putting a crown in the entire piece."

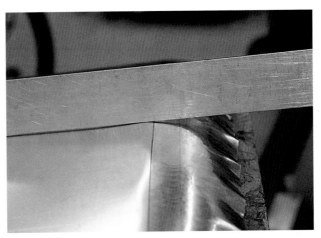

This is a look at the bottom edge after the sharper stretching dies were used to help establish the roll where the panel turns under.

The second set of stretching dies (shown at left) are used here to begin creating crown across the entire piece.

Note the amount of crown in the panel, created in just a few minutes.

...in order to create more top-to-bottom crown.

Most of the crown is side to side. Though hard to see there is some crown top-to-bottom.

Next comes a test fit.

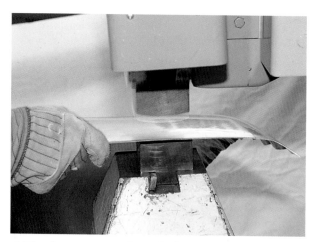

Mike does more work with the same dies...

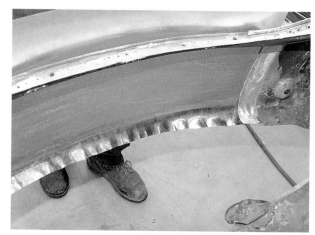

Note how close the piece is fitting when viewed from the inside.

the low spots that were left from the power hammer." With a sharper die in the planishing hammer Mike finishes the crowned area or corner at the bottom of the panel. These dies match the inside radius at that part of the panel.

Numerous test fits follow, then a change to flatter dies, now he works to finish the upper edge. The finished panel has a little more crown than the original, (when viewed the short way). But, as Mike notes, "it's hard to know how accurate the original panel was."

FOLD THE EDGE

Now the top of the old panel is clamped in place and used to draw the fold line. "Then I add close to a half inch for the folded metal even though It measures 3/8 inch," Says Mike. Then he marks a series of dashes, rolls the tape out to make a nice curved line, and cuts it with a snips.

After the piece is trimmed to fit, Mike checks the position of the fold line, then starts the folding with a pliers. "With steel I use a die on the Pullmax to score the metal, but the aluminum is so soft it's easy to over-score the metal. It's safer to just do it by hand."

Of course the lip that Mike bends into the panel tends to straighten it out, which means he needs to shrink it more. Once the crown is re-established he checks the fit again, and then bends the flange over a stake. After another test fit Mike tightens up the fold, "As you hammer the fold flat on the car, it affects the fit between the trunk lid and this panel. So it's best to get it as tight as you can before you start welding the panel in place."

The nearly finished panel is a little asymmetrical. But this is, after all, a hand built car. After comparing the new panel to the old Mike decides that the shape is true to the original so if the shape is a little unusual that's OK.

To double check the fit of the panel before the welding begins, Mike and his son Ryan set the trunk lid in place. Once it's determined that the fit of the trunk lid to the panel is good then

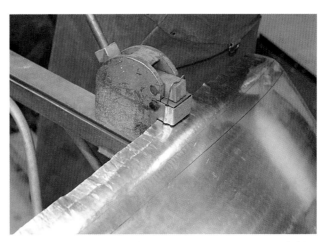

After using the power hammer to remove most of the distortion left from the thumbnail dies, Mike uses the small shrinker to tighten up the roll...

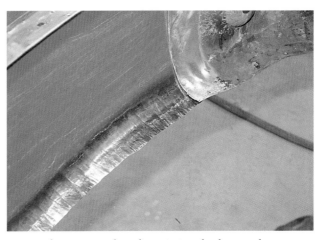

...so it better matches the existing body panels.

Now Mike can mark the panel prior to trimming and folding.

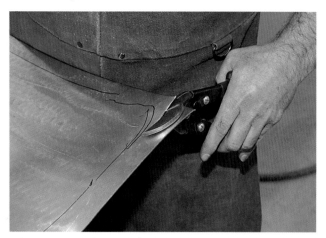

Trimming is done in various steps, followed by...

...another test fit...

...followed by finish work on the planishing hammer. This will add slightly to the panel's crown.

the trunk lid is lifted off and Mike does some minor trimming necessary to make the new panel fit.

Before welding Mike de-burrs the edges and cleans them with Acetone on a rag. The panel is welded in place with the TIG welder using a 1/16th inch pure tungsten. Mike uses a TIG welder with the amperage control on the handle not on the pedal (set at 75 amps).

Welding this piece of aluminum in place is a little difficult, partly because the original body panels are thin and partly because there is corrosion on the original panels that makes it hard to weld. During the welding, Mike notes that, "They no longer recommend forming a "ball" on the end of the tungsten when you're welding aluminum. The standards have changed."

THE FINISH WORK

When it comes to finishing the metal, Mike avoids what is commonly called metal finishing, because, "it ruins the integrity of the metal. I tend to work the metal as much as I can without doing a lot of filing. I try to leave the metal as thick as possible." He also notes that, "No matter what level you take the piece to, you're going to have to finish it more after it's in place, just because of the distortion from welding."

At this point the panel is in place, with only the finish work to do. For finishing, Mike puts crown back in with the Chicago Pneumatic air-planishing hammer. This planishing or finishing is done in two sessions, one with flat dies, the last with slightly more crowned dies.

INTERVIEW WITH MIKE PAVLETIC

Mike, can we start with some background on you and how you became a metal fabricator?

I was hired into my cousin's body shop in high school, prepping and painting cars. From there I did the route of regular body shops for five or six years, before getting into high end stuff, the high dollar European cars, the money cars. I did that for ten years. When I was working in somebody else's shop I was mostly painting. I moved home to my own shop 15 years ago. It was street rod work, I did the paint and

The work of the planishing hammer leaves Mike with a panel that is nearly perfect and correctly crowned just enough in both directions.

A test fit shows the new panel to be a very good match with the other existing panels.

Mike finished the area of maximum radius with the planishing hammer and a sharper die than what was used earlier.

A straight edge is used to check the amount of crown from top to bottom.

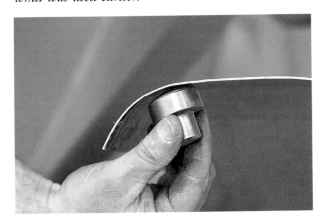

Here you can see the lower die used to finish the area seen above.

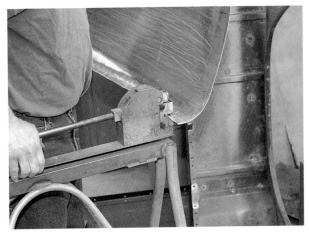

The small hand-shrinker is used to tighten up the roll slightly on the bottom of the panel.

131

At this point Mike checks the fit and the amount of crown against the original inner structure.

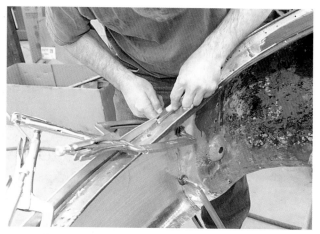

Now the piece is clamped in place so Mike can mark the fold line.

The position of the fold line, and the amount of metal to leave for the fold itself, are checked against the upper part of the "original" panel.

the whole car. Then a couple of years ago I built this building and now metal work is pretty much all I do.

I could metal finish the cars clear back when I was painting. But I wasn't hired to do metal work. I'm lucky, if I see somebody do something I can usually pick it up and that's how I learned a lot of this.

At some point you took a class from Fay Butler?

Yes, because otherwise you read magazines and books and you buy tools. Then you get an English wheel and you aren't sure how to use it. Fay can impart knowledge that you can't get acquire any place else, at least at that time you couldn't. I started to understand things like 'working past the metal's elastic limit.' Once you learn all the terms and metallurgy you know what's happening at the atomic level of the steel. Fay's a good teacher.

You said you started with a wheel and now you have a power hammer. Can you explain the advantages of each and why you bought the tools you did?

I built the wheel and learned how to use it, I didn't think it was that difficult to use. Then I went to Fay's and saw his power hammers and saw that was more efficient. So then I sold the English wheel and bought a power hammer. I tell a lot of guys to buy a wheel. It's affordable, you can wheel out a panel and have it nice and not need any filler. Some of the schools are starting to cover the use of a wheel. You supply all the power to the wheel though, with a power hammer you use the motor to supply the force.

Now you do most of your work on a power hammer?

Yes, it's a tremendous tool. Part of it is learning the use of the hammer. Instead of hammering a fender over a sand bag and then smoothing it out with a wheel, you can shape it nice and easy with the hammer. Most of the pieces I make don't even need to be planished.

What's the minimum tooling a person needs to do advanced-level shaping?

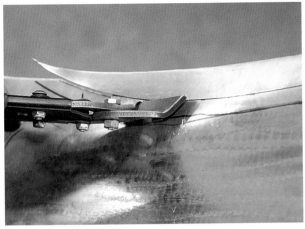

Here you can see both the fold line and the trim line.

Before finishing up the fold with a hammer working over a stake.

Mike's son Chase steadies the panel as the beginning of the fold is formed by hand.

The panel can now be slid down into place...

To re-create some of the crown, Mike runs the folded area through the hand shrinker.

...before being welded to the other panels with the TIG welder.

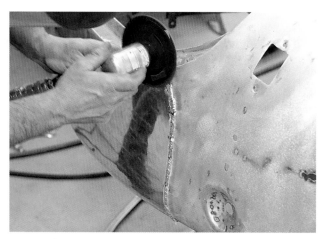

A grinder and coarse disc are used to do the first step in finishing the welded seam...

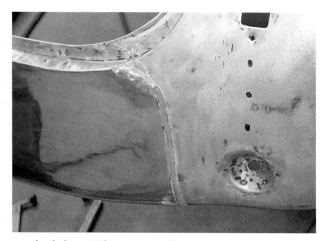

...which leaves the seam in the condition seen here. The other effect of the welding is to eliminate some of the top-to-bottom crown.

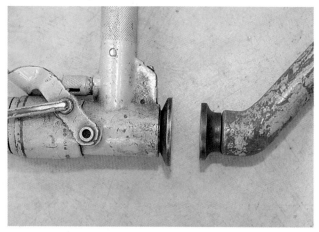

To finish the seam and re-crown the panel Mike uses an air planishing hammer equipped initially with fairly flat dies (shown), then with more crowned dies.

An English wheel and a Pullmax would be a good start. And some kind of welder.

Bigger pieces mean more seams, is a TIG welder essential?

You don't have to have a TIG welder. Lots of guys only have gas welders and they do fine. The TIG makes things easier. It's a matter of what you've learned and what you can afford. The gas weld is annealed so it's soft and you can hammer-weld it and end up with a nice seam. I started with a Dillon gas-welding outfit. It only uses 4-5 pounds of pressure for both gasses so you're less likely to blow through when you're welding aluminum.

What about bucks, how often do you use one?

I personally don't have the type of jobs that need a buck. I don't use them very often. Part of it depends on the work that comes through your door. They have a place, but they're not always a necessity.

Advanced Sheet metal means bigger more complex shapes. Can you talk about the seams. How does a person decide where to put the seams and how does he or she decide how many pieces to make an individual part out of?

That should probably be determined by the size of the panel and the access you have to the area where you want to put the seam. I'm inclined to put them in a crowned area rather than a flat area. The crowned area has more strength, it won't warp as much and you can run the planishing hammer over it when you're done. Basically, it comes down to your skill level.

Aluminum and steel, do you prefer one over the other?

Depends on what it is. Whatever work I get, that's what I do. The Alfa is aluminum, I don't have a problem with either one.

Is there one skill that's more important than the others?

You need a whole combination of skills. On a personal level, you need the drive to do it. You work with yourself so you have to be a good problem solver.

Is a good eye essential to metal shaping?

Yes, definitely. If you look at something and it doesn't look right it probably isn't. You need to make a correction. I tell my sons, "if it looks right it is right."

Are there abilities that hold people back from bigger projects. Where do people fall down in terms of skills or abilities?

There's really only two things, the experience of doing it and the knowledge. It helps to get the knowledge at a seminar or from a book. Then you have to apply it. If a person is trying to learn it too quick. if they read all these books and then just want to run out and start making panels then they can get in over their head. The more knowledge you can acquire, the quicker the learning curve is.

Don't expect to be able to do it as well as someone who's done it for 20 years. Set your goals high but not so high that you fail. Give your self time to learn. Be patient, it doesn't happen overnight.

The small air planishing hammer is designed to he hand-held so panels can be finished on the car.

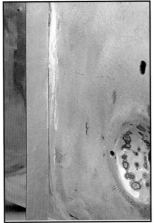

Before and after shots use a ruler to show how much crown the panel picked us as a result of Mike's work with the hand-held planishing hammer.

The old Alfa with the "patch panel" installed. Though the gauge and alloy used in the new panel are very close to the old panels, it was still hard to weld, due to inevitable corrosion and inconsistencies in the thickness of the original metal.

Chapter Seven - Bob Munroe

Turbine Power

A New Rocket from Arlen Ness

The new Arlen Ness turbine-powered bike started life as a rendering drawn up by artist Carl Brouhard. "I was ready for something different," explains Arlen, "I try to do one really wild bike each year and this is it. Jay Leno has one and it looks like a sport bike, I decided to make this bike look like a jet."

Arlen is quick to point out the differences between his bike and any other "jet" bikes. "One of the big things we did is install an electric motor.

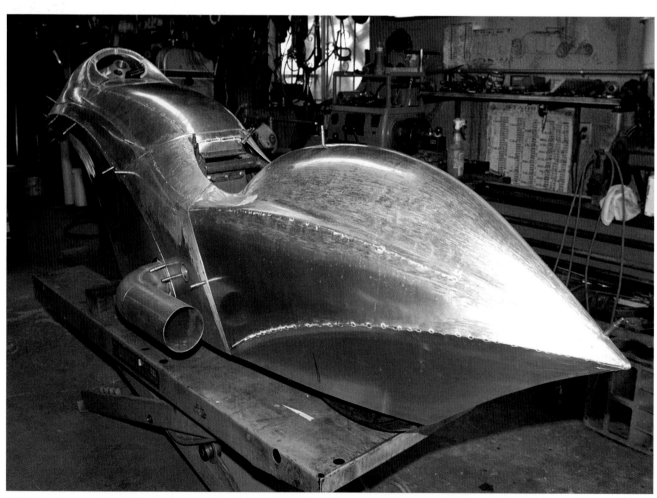

This is the complete bike with just a little more work to be do. The tail section and middle panels are formed but not finished. The seat area needs to be rolled up and fit as well.

You can't ride turbines when there's people around, they give off so much heat. The engine runs on 24 volts, so we put in two 12 volt Optima batteries, wired in series, and hooked them up to a golf cart motor. I can ride it around town on the electric motor and never have to fire the jet engine."

The engine is an AP 110 gas turbine engine, retired from active military service. Fitting the engine into the confines of a motorcycle frame meant building a custom frame, a job that fell to Bob Monroe, the same man responsible for the very nice sheet metal work.

Known in motorcycle circles as "The Mun," or simply, "Mun," Bob Munroe is responsible for more award winning Arlen Ness sheet metal than any other individual. Bob started out building frames and exhaust systems for Arlen during Arlen's early years, and soon graduated to sheet metal fabrication. Working out of a small shop with hand tools and an English wheel, Bob Monroe is capable of forming steel or aluminum panels that are both well crafted and stunning to behold.

"This was such a big project that I really didn't know where to start on the body panels," explains Bob. "I spent a lot of time looking at the sketches, finally I started on the two big side covers and just worked from there."

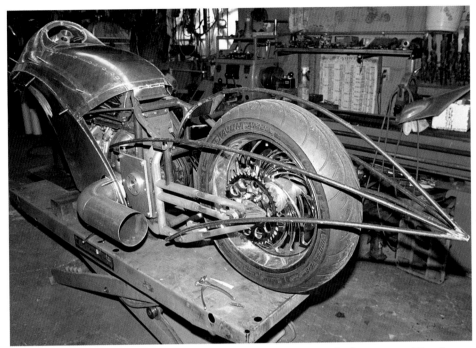

An overview part way through the project. The front of bike is roughed in complete with side pieces, the nose, and gas tank cover. The frame work for the tail section is designed to be removable to allow service of the rear wheel. The outer skin will fasten to that cage work.

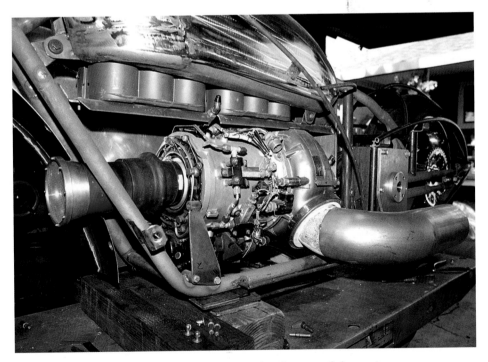

The business end of this unusual motorcycle. On top of the engine are two Optima batteries, and on top of that a six gallon gas tank formed from aluminum designed to stretch over the batteries.

As we go to press the bike is essentially finished, with only the seat pan and the finish work to do. When asked, Bob says he doesn't plan to edge-wire the bike, "Because it would take so long, the bike has so many edges. And it's mostly an exhibition bike, it won't get ridden a lot of miles. I will edge-wire anything Arlen wants me to, but I think I'll just double the metal at the edges and leave it at that."

A short mini-sequence. Bob wheels the center part of the gas tank cover after roughing it out on the bag first. All the panels are made from 3003, H14, aluminum, .063 Inches thick.

All photos supplied by Jonathan Gold

After the wheeling Bob scribes a line to provide clearance for the forks when the bike is turned. The gas tank cover will be three pieces, this is the center piece.

Now he trims off the excess aluminum.

One more session on the wheel to further smooth and finish the panel. Bob still has to fit the two smaller panels to complete the gas tank cover.

After tack welding the three pieces together Bob goes back to the wheel to get everything back into shape. He describes this as, "gentle light wheeling."

Here he's fitting the center panel to the two thin side pieces attached to the bike with cleco clamps.

After the wheeling it's time for a test fit.

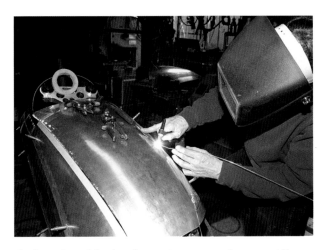

Bob tack welds the three pieces to make one. All welds are done with the heli-arc and Bob does his tack welds every half inch.

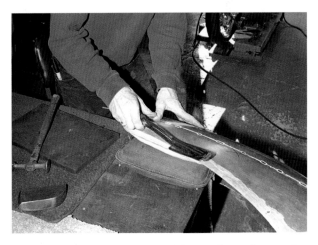

Bob says he's, "Working the edge with my bag and slapper, it was too loose, so I'm tightening that up a little."

With a bead roller and the right dies Bob steps the back of the gas tank cover so the next piece will overlap with a flush fit.

Part way through the project Arlen and Bob take time to assess the progress of this very complex project.

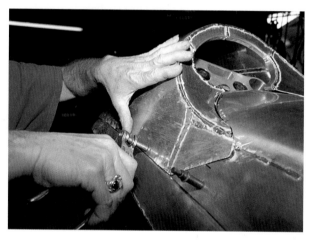

Here you can see how the other panels fit up against the gas tank cover and why it was necessary to create the stepped edge.

The tail section, seen here nearly completed, is designed to come off the bike as a sub-assembly.

The top of rear fender after Bob has it roughed out. "I bagged it and used the shrinker on the sides and did some wheeling."

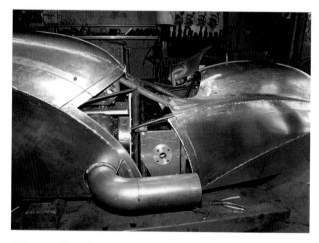

The small side panels and seat pan are the last things Bob made for the bike.

The wheel is used to smooth out the side cover on the exhaust side.

Now the cover is fastened in place. The finished exhaust pipe, and heat shields(!), will be made from stainless due to the heat.

The right side view shows off the finished bike with a certain amount of welding and a lot of finish work still to do. Bob says he, "Annealed everything that has a lot of shape, the top of the tank and rear fender and most of the front panels. The rest of it doesn't call for it, there's not that much shape."

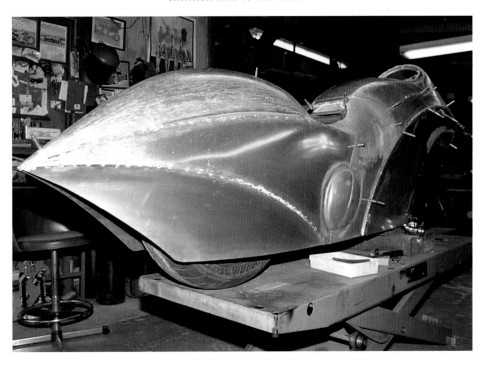

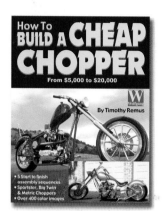

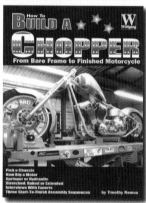

HOW TO BUILD A CHEAP CHOPPER

Choppers don't have to cost $30,000. In fact, a chopper built from the right parts can be assembled for as little as $5,000. *How to Build a Cheap Chopper* documents the construction of 4 inexpensive choppers with complete start-to-finish sequences photographed in the shops of Tom Summers, Donnie Smith, Brian Klock and Dave Perewitz.

Least expensive is the metric chopper, based on a Japanese 4-cylinder engine and transmission installed in an hardtail frame. Next up, price wise, are 2 bikes built using Buell/Sportster drivetrains. The recipe here is simple, combine one used Buell or Sportster with a hardtail frame for an almost instant chopper. The big twin chopper is the least cheap of the 4, yet it's still far less expensive than most bikes built today.

Twelve Chapters   144 Pages $24.95   Over 400 photos-100% color

HOW TO BUILD A CHOPPER

Designed to help you build your own chopper, this book covers History, Frames, Chassis Components, Wheels and Tires, Engine Options, Drivetrains, Wiring, Sheet Metal and Hardware. Included are assembly sequences from the Arlen Ness, Donnie Smith and American Thunder shops. Your best first step! Order today.

Choppers are back! Learn from the best how to build yours.
12 chapters cover:
- Use of Evo, TC, Shovel, Pan or Knucklehead engines
- Frame and running gear choices
- Design decisions - short and stubby or long and radical?
- Four, five or six-speed trannies

Twelve Chapters   144 Pages $24.95   Over 300 photos-over 50% color

ADVANCED AIRBRUSH ART

Like a video done with still photography, this new book from Wolfgang Publications is made up entirely of photo sequences that illustrate each small step in the creation of an airbrushed masterpiece. Watch as well-known masters like Vince Goodeve, Chris Cruz, Steve Wizard and Nick Pastura start with a sketch and end with a NASCAR helmet or motorcycle tank covered with graphics, murals, pinups or all of the above.

Interviews explain each artist's preference for paint and equipment, and secrets learned over decades of painting. Projects include a chrome eagle surrounded by reality flames, a series of murals, and a variety of graphic designs.
Color images explain each step necessary for the creation of a masterful airbrushed image. This is a great book for anyone who takes their airbrushing seriously and wants to learn more.

Ten Chapters   144 Pages $24.95   Over 500 photos - 100% color

PRO AIRBRUSH TECHNIQUES WITH VINCE GOODEVE

Written by well-known Airbrush artist Vince Goodeve, this new book uses 144 pages and over 500 color images to explain a lifetime's worth of learning. Follow Vince through multiple photo sequences that explain his choice of color, sense of design and preference for tools and materials. Early chapters explain shop set up and preparations of the metal canvas. Fifteen start-to-finish sequences

walk the reader through Vince's airbrush work with both motorcycles and cars. Projects include simple graphics as well as complex and intricate designs. Accustomed to teaching, Vince uses a style that is easy to follow and understand. His enthusiasm for the airbrush comes through, making the text easy to follow. Vince Goodeve has something to say to all airbrush artists – whether beginner or advanced.

Fifteen Chapters   144 Pages $24.95   Over 400 photos, 10% color

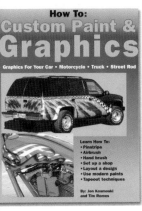

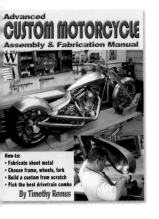

Sources

Cal Davis
Metal Craft Tools
431 Linda St
Macclenny, FL 32063
904-259-4427
Metalcrafttools.com
Metal Craft offers a power
hammer kit, as well as an
English wheel, various hand
tools and shaping classes to
boot.

Centaur Forge LTD
117 No Spring St
PO Box 340
Burlington, WI 53105
262-763-9175
Centaur Forge offers a unique
catalog filled with everything
from books on metal working
to complete air hammers.
Though much of the catalog is
given over to horseshoes and
related products, there's also a
wealth of unique tools and
books sure to interest the sheet
metal craftsman.

Covell Creative Metalworking
106 Airport Blvd. Unit 105
Freedom CA 95019
toll-free number
800-747-4631
831-768-0705
website: www.covell.biz

Clay Cook
Phone: 606-282-7545

Craig Naff
1199 Stultz Gap Road
Woodstock, VA 22664
540-459-3394
Donnie Smith Custom Cycle
Rob Roehl
10594 Raddison Rd NE
Blaine, MN 55449
763-786-6002
Fax:763-786-0660

Fay Butler
Fab/Metal Shaping
51 Cleveland Rd
Wheelwright, MA 01094
413-477-6449
fayfab@mindspring.com
Fay offers his seminars, does
consulting and also manufac-
tures tooling and books.

Gulley Performance Center
2604 Fort Henry Dr.
Kingsport, TN 37664
jgulley59@earthlink.net
Gulley Performance sells
a variety of metal shaping tools
and equipment

Loren Richards Tooling
928 636 2625
Chino Valley, AZ 86323
loren910@cableone.net

www.metalshapers.org
A great source of ideas, inspira-
tion and help from a wide
variety of well-known names in
metal shaping.

Michigan Pneumatic
800-521-8104
313-933-5890
FAX: 313-933-0440
michiganpneumatic.com
Good source of air planishing
hammers, parts and dies.

Neal's Custom Metal
3023 104th Ln. NE
Blaine, MN 55449
763-210-0633
FAX: 763-506-0288

Mike Pavletic Fabrications
12885 21st St
Beach Park, IL 60099
choptop1970@aol.com

Precision Metal
Fab & Machine
Jim Hervatin
22789 NW Service Rd.
Warrenton, MO 63383
636-456-7242
Fax: 636-456-4808
Jim has a variety of parts for
Yoder power hammers, and also
makes a set of steel sweeps.

TCE Corporation
P.O. Box 330056
West Hartford, CT 06133
1-800-886-2611

Yoder
26800 Richmond Rd
Cleveland, OH 44146
800-631-0520